A
YEAR OF
SCOTTISH
POEMS

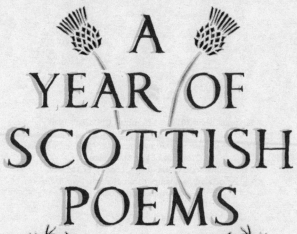

A YEAR OF SCOTTISH POEMS

FOREWORD BY JACKIE KAY

CHOSEN BY
GABY MORGAN

MACMILLAN

First published 2018 by Macmillan Children's Books

This edition published 2020 by Macmillan Children's Books
an imprint of Pan Macmillan
The Smithson, 6 Briset Street, London EC1M 5NR
Associated companies throughout the world
www.panmacmillan.com

ISBN 978-1-5290-0825-8

1 3 5 7 9 8 6 4 2

A CIP catalogue record for this book is available from the British Library.

Poems chosen by Gaby Morgan
Typset by The Dimpse
Glossary by Gillian Hamnett

Printed and bound by CPI Group (UK) Ltd, Croydon

For all the islanders, highlanders,
lowlanders and my very own outlanders

– Gaby

Contents

February

March

April

June

July

August

September

October

November

December

Foreword

Every Hogmanay* throughout the world the words of an eighteenth century poem are sung. Robert Burns, the author of 'Auld Lang Syne', is the only poet who is celebrated with his own day, Burns Day, on the 25th of January. Not even Shakespeare is accorded this honour.

Poetry, both oral and written, is the national art of Scotland. From John Barbour to Liz Lochhead, Scots poets have reflected and responded to their landscape – rural or industrial – to their various languages, to the history of Caledonia and to their changing relationships, both personal and political. We hear the voice of our passionate, proud and provocative country most truly in its poetry. And we get a sense of the breadth and the width of our land in all its shimmering lights and differing guises, its whole tonal and vocal range. There are poems in this enlivening anthology that mirror the country's dynamic and beautiful landscape, poems that tell the time.

A Year of Scottish Poems creates a winning and complex portrait of today's Scotland as well as yesterday's. It is an anthology that opens the croft door and the tenement one. There are poems here that will strike a chord of recognition whether you are from Scotland or simply love Scotland, poems that will make you go 'aww', as well as poems to make you greet or laugh.

In this Scottish poetic calendar poems tell time's stories from January to December in the most interesting of ways. Some poems are dead certs for obvious days: 'Address to a Haggis', 'Auld Lang Syne', 'The Loch Ness Monster's Song' on the 1st April, 'Fireworks aff the Castle' on the 5th November,

*New Year's Eve

xxiii

'When You See Millions of the Mouthless Dead' on Armistice day, but others fit to the day in less tied ways. Here poems cross the entire year to remind us why we love the seasons and the rituals around special days.

These poems also vary hugely in form and type – from the witty to the sardonic, the sing-songy to the ironic, the satirical to the lyrical, from the dramatic monologue to the sonnet, the haiku to the tender love poem, *A Year of Scottish Poems* gives you an entire elevating range.

Here's a book that lets you get to know a year differently, through voices new and old, well kent and anon, past and present. For a small country, Scotland holds its own in poetry and all parts of Scotland have poetic roots. The reader gets a real sense of just how democratic this poetry anthology is – each voice is here with its clear pitch, its own tone, its vision. A poem is a little moment of belief. This book places Scotland firmly on planet poetry, flying you there and back in a single day.

A Year of Scottish Poems is full of personalities – their voices, their peculiarities, loveable and funny, crabbit and wabbit – a whole cast of characters for all times. And the character of the landscape is ever present, relit and reinvented by voices across the centuries, lovingly depicting the nooks and crannies, the secret places. Poetry itself is a secret place and a wide open one; it welcomes the pioneer and the adventurer. An anthology like this takes you on a journey across Scotland and across time to capture the small and complex country that is home to a whole panorama of poets. Enjoy!

Jackie Kay

January

I

Hello, I am Scotland

Who wakes every morning
in a brilliant mood as auburn bursts
cast filigree nets over foreheads
and swingparks and paint themselves
on pavements. Up gets the brickworks,
frost needles arms, winds shriek
through my Munros, gossiping
as another small dug sinks
into deep snow; and the day floats down
like a feather from the sky. Ach,
barks a father's voice caught
in the breeze, let him sing
his song and paint whitever it is
he cares tae paint. I've a soft spot fur daft
romantics and who wouldnae
grasp for it, when it really could be it.

My cities breathe in the rivers,
salute the environmentalists: snail
savers, wall walkers, ally
of Elm and Ash. Every day my oceans
swallow five hundred thousand footprints,
strangle gulls in fitted laughter,
emit the salty corpse; seasplash
spears a drunken busker
mixing up his cluster chords.

I, too, forget such simple things,
perhaps have never known
all the numbers of the buses
and their routes, the vagaries in roadworks;
but I do remember bonfires
in aw them bellies as whole families
politicised breakfast over toasted soldiers
and eggs unfit and fit for dipping.

We jumped without parachutes,
so they'd have you think (skirted
around each other's glances
like window cleaners avoiding
a high-up mucky splodge); it wasn't that
at all, more a faith in flying.

Michael Pedersen

2

Promise

Remember, the time of year
when the future appears
like a blank sheet of paper
a clean calendar, a new chance.
On thick white snow

you vow fresh footprints
then watch them go
with the wind's hearty gust.
Fill your glass. Here's tae us. Promises
made to be broken, made to last.

Jackie Kay

3

Chaudhri Sher Mobarik looks at the loch

Light shakes out the dishrag sky
and scatters the water with sequins. *Look, hen!*
says my father, *Loch Lomond!* as if
it were all his doing, as if he owned it,
laird of Lomond, laird of the language.
He is proud to say *hen* and even more *loch*
with an *och* not an *ock*, to speak
proper Glaswegian like a true-born Scot,
and he makes the right sound at the back
of the throat because he can say *khush*
and *khwab* and *khamosh*, because the sounds
for happy and dream are the words that swim
in the water for him, so he says it again,
Hen! Look! The loch!

Imtiaz Dharker

4

Recreation

She makes embroidery
As bees make honey
From flowers and colours.

It absorbs her.
She is drawn by threads
Into the heart of the pattern.

In the slipping, bitty
Ripples of domesticity
She likes the sedentary

Intricate necessity
Of this embroidery.
It must be just so, exactly,

And yet can wait, not spoiling,
Not boiling over, when
She lays it down (for cries

Of children, phone, kettle).
She rises, goes
To do whatever she has to

And returns to the quiet tugging
Of thread, unbroken,
Piecing together (when she has a moment)

Complete, unwithering roses.

Elma Mitchell

5

Friends

It showed how friendship
doesn't end (like when
Emma and I watched

eight episodes in one go)
though outside my window
the climate was changing

and in my experience
people found each other
quite easy to take or leave.

The day after the last episode
they ran them all again,
protecting me, it seems.

I keep just one from
two-hundred-and-thirty-six.
It's the one where Ross says,

but this can't be it,
and Rachel says,
then how come it is?

and he sinks to his knees with his arms
around her legs and the camera
moves slowly back

and they hold the shot
for a long time
before the theme tune begins.

Polly Clark

6

Queen o the Bean

Mary Fleming, 1542–1581, Scotland; relative, childhood
companion and lady-in-waiting to Mary Queen of Scots;
on Uphaly Nicht – the Feast of Epiphany – in 1563, Mary
Fleming was the lucky one to get the piece of traditional
King Cake (Black Bun) with the bean concealed in it, and
so was 'Queen of the Bean' for the night.

Yon wis a ploy! In ma mindin fur aye.
It stairtit at breakfast, wi cake – she couldnae wait.
We were sat up in bed thegither (ever sin I claucht
thon cuif o a French poet hid in her chaumer, fired up
fur hoochmagandie, we'd slept side by side);
'Noo, ma douce wee cuz,' says oor Lady Queen,
gien me the ashet, 'tak a bite o Black Bun,
an let's see if ye'll beir the gree!' I sink ma teeth
intae crisp pastry crust, syne hinnie faulds o moist daurk –
raisons, cinnamon, almonds, citrus, ginger, as if
the essence o thae gifts the Three Kings
brocht tae Christ are fluidin ower ma tongue's buds;
and then it comes – the haurd, leamin surface
agin ma gums – the bean! An her lauch like licht
fills the mornin: 'Ye will be Queen this Uphaly Nicht!'
says she, awready oot o bed, rakin through her kist
o treisurs – they're skailin tae the flair in a skinklin spate.
'I'll hae ye geared up sae braw, ma Mary dear,
ye wull cherm the hale court – a glisterin spreet
o Christmastide ye sall be, nae maitter that Maister Knox

hus bainished it frae the almanac; I wull mak ye
a merrie Phoenix that wull rise afore us aa!'

Och, ye shoud hae seen me, tho I say it masel –
I wis braw! She hud me happed in a siller goon,
Orient stanes threidit through ma braidit hair,
dreepin frae ma broo, ma halse, ma paps –
ma hale form a veesion in amethyst an jade,
emerant, amber, topaz, an a sash o sapphires, blue
as the dawn ower Bethlehem; bangles o gowd,
pearls like snawdraps, rubies reid as Rizzio's bluid.

Bluid. Ower muckle o't hus syped awa
doon the years sin syne, thae daffin days
o licht-hertit ploys. The warld is grey an mirk,
a wanlit place withoot a braith o colour tae its face,
nae feastin noo, nae dancin, guisin, liftin o the hert
in sang; oor anely solace fur the saul is kennin we hae
lauched thegither, lauched sin we were careless bairns
in a blurr o bluebell wids on haly Inchmaholm; lauched
as lasses, at the lottery o it aa, the castin o the die:
Queen fur aiblins hauf a hunder year,
or ae ferlie nicht, fur juist a blink.

Gerda Stevenson

7

Enquiry Desk

Scottish Poetry Library

Do you have the one
with that poem they read at the funeral
in that movie?

Do you have the one
with that poem that they used to make us
learn at secondary school?

Do you have the one
with that poem that the Librarians decided was
too beautiful to catalogue and classify?

Do you have the one
with that poem that knows the difference between
ae thing and *anither thing*?

Do you have the one
with that poem that sat in the corner for ten years and then
exploded like a grenade in a crowded space?

Do you have the one
with that poem from the box of love letters
the city keeps under its bed?

Do you have the one
with that poem that identifies the chemical properties
of the ghosts of ideas it contains?

Do you have the one
with that poem that is a cache of weapons
which can never be put beyond use?

Do you have the one
with that poem that has learned to impersonate
other poems it has never met?

Do you have the one
with that poem that has mastered chiaroscuro
yet can also emulsion a room in an hour?

Do you have the one
with that poem that stole into my lover's bed
when I wasn't reading it?

Do you have the one
with that poem that is bigger on the inside
than on the outside?

Do you have the one
    – you must have it –
    with that poem that is a Library in itself,
    each leaf a life we might one day live?

I don't know what it's called
but it calls, it calls.

Andy Jackson

8

Extremely Large Telescope

We listen at the door of the room,
the Universe has just made its grand
entrance, the energetic reception
flattens the walls, creates new dimensions.

A jazz band is getting ready to play
the next number, wiping spit
from its mouthpiece; expectation
has its own gravitational pull.

So this is a night, the first one, already
cooling. But the crowd still expanding, pushing out.

Light plays the darling, rumouring
through the crowd. We watch it shrink
to hear-say; histories glint in glass eyes.

The lone note of a trumpet drifts
down between the years, its wave and
bounce barely stirring the bluesy smoke.

This far back everything shimmers.
We must get here earlier next time, we say,
as the Universe milks faint applause.

Vicki Husband

9

Scottish Haiku

A bonny Ayrshire
chews the cud on Ben Nevis –
noo *that's* a high coo!

John Rice

10

Kidspoem / Bairnsang

it wis January
and a gey dreich day
the first day Ah went to the school
so my Mum happed me up in ma
good navy-blue napp coat wi the rid tartan hood
birled a scarf aroon ma neck
pu'ed oan ma pixie an my pawkies
it wis that bitter
said *noo ye'll no starve*
gie'd me a wee kiss and a kid-oan skelp oan the bum
and sent me aff across the playground
tae the place Ah'd learn to say
it was January
and a really dismal day
the first day I went to school
so my mother wrapped me up in my
best navy-blue top coat with the red tartan hood
twirled a scarf around my neck
pulled on my bobble-hat and mittens
it was so bitterly cold
said *now you won't freeze to death*
gave me a little kiss and a pretend slap on the bottom
and sent me off across the playground
to the place I'd learn to forget to say
it wis January
and a gey dreich day
the first day Ah went to the school

so my Mum happed me up in ma
good navy-blue napp coat wi the rid tartan hood
birled a scarf aroon ma neck
pu'ed oan ma pixie an ma pawkies
it wis that bitter.

Oh saying it was one thing
but when it came to writing it
in black and white
the way it had to be said
was as if you were posh, grown-up, male, English and dead.

Liz Lochhead

11

Brendon Gallacher

For my brother, Maxie

He was seven and I was six, my Brendon Gallacher.
He was Irish and I was Scottish, my Brendon Gallacher.
His father was in prison; he was a cat burglar.
My father was a communist party full-time worker.
He had six brothers and I had one, my Brendon Gallacher.

He would hold my hand and take me by the river
Where we'd talk all about his family being poor.
He'd get his mum out of Glasgow when he got older.
A wee holiday some place nice. Some place far.
I'd tell my mum about my Brendon Gallacher.

How his mum drank and his daddy was a cat burglar.
And she'd say, 'why not have him round to dinner?'
No, no, I'd say, he's got big holes in his trousers.
I like meeting him by the burn in the open air.
Then one day after we'd been friends two years,

One day when it was pouring and I was indoors,
My mum says to me, 'I was talking to Mrs Moir
Who lives next door to your Brendon Gallacher
Didn't you say his address was 24 Novar?
She says there are no Gallachers at 24 Novar

There never have been any Gallachers next door.'
And he died then, my Brendon Gallacher,
Flat out on my bedroom floor, his spiky hair,
His impish grin, his funny flapping ear.
Oh Brendon, Oh my Brendon Gallacher.

Jackie Kay

12

Bobbie Shafto

Bobbie Shafto's gane tae sea,
Siller buckles on his knee,
He'll come back an mairry me,
Bonny Bobbie Shafto.

Anon.

13

from A Bard's Address to His Youngest Daughter

Come to my arms my wee wee pet
My mild my blithesome Harriet
The sweetest babe art thou to me
That ever sat on parent's knee.
Thou hast that eye was mine erewhile
Thy mother's blithe and grateful smile
And such a playful merry vein
That greybeards smile at pranks of thine

And if aright I read thy mind
The child of nature thou'rt designed
For even while yet upon the breast
Thou mimic'st child and bird and beast
Can'st cry like Moggy o'er her book
And crow like cock and caw like rook
Boo like a bull and blare like ram
And bark like dog and bleat like lamb
And when abroad in pleasant weather
Thou minglest all these sounds together
Then who can say, thou happy creature,
Thou'rt not the very child of nature

How dar'st thou frown, thou freakish fay,
And pout and look the other way?
Why turn thy chubby cheeks athraw
And skelp the beard of thy papa?
I know full well thy deep design
'Tis to turn back thine eye on mine
With triple burst of joyful glee
And fifty strains at mimicry
What wealth from nature may'st thou won
With pupilage so soon begun.
Well, hope is all; thou art unproved,
The bard's and nature's best beloved.
And now above thy brow so fair
And flowing films of flaxen hair
I lay my hand once more and frame
A blessing in the holy name
Of that supreme divinity
Who breathed a living soul in thee.

James Hogg

14

All the Clouds

And it would be simpler to contain all the clouds
in a single jar unlidded
than expect this love to be returned.
Just as the wind – breathless – carries a song
and never quietens its bustle to listen,
just as a bird's shadow streams over a lake,
just as our country exists and it doesn't,
and just as our world's original dawn
will never again equal itself, but rises blushing
that it be admired as a constant failing,
so you are here and are not here,
your face a bright mist in my dreams gently fading.

Kevin MacNeil

15

Three wee craws sat upon a wa'

Three wee craws sat upon a wa'
  sat upon a wa', sat upon a wa'.
Three wee craws sat upon a wa'
  on a cold and frosty morning.

The first wee craw couldnae flee at a'
  couldnae flee at a', couldnae flee at a'.
The first wee craw couldnae flee at a'
  on a cold and frosty morning.

The second wee craw wis greetin' fur his maw
  greetin' fur his maw, greetin' fur his maw.
The second wee craw wis greetin' fur his maw
  on a cold and frosty morning.

The third wee craw wisnae there at a'
  wisnae there at a', wisnae there at a'.
The third wee craw wisnae there at a'
  on a cold and frosty morning.

Anon.

16

Two Saints

My first school was a wooden bungalow
named for Brigid, patron saint of wells.
I thought she must be cold, like the closed spring
that whispered in the wood behind our house,
but later I was told of sacred fires
deep in Kildare, where monasteries were built
according to Pope Gregory's decree.
The elder Brigid glimmered in that land:
a motion under flames, the shifting greens
of dark and bright, bound in a speaking hearth.
I felt time shatter when the Normans came.

Lessons went unlearned. I played a part,
scratched the twelve times table on my cuffs
and copied spelling lists from hidden books.
But I was thinking of the undergrowth.
There would be dreams and Brigid would be there;
blue as rain her firelight on my skin.

One day I helped my father clear a pond.
We drew rakes through the water, gathered weed
and raised it dripping, shot with sudden light.
The weft was heavy, tugging for its depth.
Spread on the path, it shone like new-dyed silk.

That year we moved. There was another school:
red brick walls, locks and window bars.
It echoed like a vault when we ran out
to Christmases; the waxy corridors
swarmed with Roman numerals and names.
Saint Columba's High. If there were tales
of wicker furnaces and holy wells
I have forgotten them.
Every month we had a class exam:
History was statute books and wars,
Sixteen Hundred to the present day,
never reaching now. I started French.
All I knew of that school's saint was this:
that it was he who gave the people
books and silence at the story's end
and on an island sheltered from the stream
he drowned the oracles in chiselled stone.

John Burnside

17

The world is busy, Katie

The world is busy, Katie, and tonight
the planes are playing, fine, alright, but soon
the folk behind those blinks will nap, sleep tight,
as you will too, beneath a nitelite moon.
The world is busy, Katie, but it's late –
the trains are packing up, the drunks are calm.
The fast, the slow, has gone. It's only freight
that storms the garage lane. It means no harm.
The world is busy, Katie, but it's dark –
the lorries nod, they snort, they spoil their chrome.
They hate to be alone. For them, a lay-by's home.
The world is busy, Katie, like I said,
but *you're* the world – and tired. It's time for bed.

Richard Price

18

Whit's in there?

Whit's in there?
Gowd an money.
Whaur's my share o't?
The moosie ran awa wi't.
Whaur's the moosie?
In her hoosie.
Whaur's her hoosie?
In the wid.
Whaur's the wid?
The fire burnt it.
Whaur's the fire?
The watter quencht it.
Whaur's the watter?
The broon bull drank it.
Whaur's the broon bull?
Back o' Burnie's Hill.
Whaur's Burnie's Hill?
A' claid wi snaw.
Whaur's the snaw?
The sun meltit it.
Whaur's the sun?
Heigh, heigh up i the air.

Anon.

19

Viking Boy

a sandstorm strips the dune
to bare-bones
on a straw mat
over a bed of feathers
the boy lies
a hoop of metal
shelters his head
the shield over his face
the sword by his flank
he has a bone comb
not a yellow hair in it
the bed to soften
the blow to the boy
the shield to hide
his young face
from the sharp scatter
from the first handful of sand

Valerie Gillies

20

To Anybody At All

I didn't want you cosy and neat and limited.
I didn't want you to be understandable,
Understood.
I wanted you to stay mad and limitless,
Neither bound to me nor bound to anyone else's or
    your own preconceived idea of yourself.

Margaret Tait

21

The Book of the World

Of this fair volume which we World do name
If we the sheets and leaves could turn with care,
Of him who it corrects and did it frame,
We clear might read the art and wisdom rare:
Find out his power which wildest powers doth tame,
His providence existing everywhere,
His justice which proud rebels doth not spare,
In every page, no, period of the same.
But silly we, like foolish children, rest
Well pleased with coloured vellum, leaves of gold,
Fair dangling ribands, leaving what is best,
On the great writer's sense ne'er taking hold;
Or if by chance our minds do muse on aught,
It is some picture on the margin wrought.

William Drummond of Hawthornden

22

Sisters

Even when she moved
five hundred miles away
telepathy was alive between them
and love as strong as ever

She sends in the post
pressed tulip petals
slivers of shell from the day at the beach
wrapped in tissue paper

She, a book of stories
golden earrings

and she, the painting of a windy day
the daffodil bowl

Even before the letter
saying, between the lines, 'come',
she is on her way

Elizabeth Burns

23

Johnny, come lend me yer fiddle

Johnny, come lend me yer fiddle,
If ever ye mean tae thrive.
O no, I'll no lend ma fiddle
Tae ony man alive.

Johnny sall hae a blue bonnet,
An Johnny sall gae tae the fair,
An Johnny sall hae a new ribbon,
Tae tie up his bonny broon hair.

And why shudny A love Johnny?
And why shudny Johnny love me?
And why shudny A love Johnny,
As weel as anither bodie?

An here is a leg for a stockin,
An here is a fit for a shoe,
An here is a kiss for his daddy,
An twa for his mammy, I true.

Anon.

24

Selkirk Grace

Some hae meat and canna eat,
And some wad eat that want it;
But we hae meat, and we can eat,
Sae let the Lord be thankit.

Robert Burns

25

Address to a Haggis

Fair fa' your honest, sonsie face,
Great Chieftain o' the Puddin-race!
Aboon them a' ye tak your place,
    Painch, tripe, or thairm:
Weel are ye wordy o' a *grace*
    As lang's my arm.

The groaning trencher there ye fill,
Your hurdies like a distant hill,
Your *pin* wad help to mend a mill
    In time o' need,
While thro' your pores the dews distil
    Like amber bead.

His knife see Rustic-labour dight,
An' cut you up wi' ready slight,
Trenching your gushing entrails bright,
    Like onie ditch;
And then, O what a glorious sight,
    Warm-reekin, rich!

Then, horn for horn, they stretch an' strive:
Deil tak the hindmost, on they drive,
Till a' their weel-swall'd kytes belyve
    Are bent like drums;
Then auld Guidman, maist like to rive,
    Bethankit hums.

Is there that owre his French *ragout*,
Or *olio* that wad staw a sow,
Or *fricassee* wad mak her spew
   Wi' perfect scunner,
Looks down wi' sneering, scornfu' view
   On sic a dinner?

Poor devil! see him owre his trash,
As feckless as a wither'd rash,
His spindle shank a guid whip-lash,
   His nieve a nit;
Thro' bluidy flood or field to dash,
   O how unfit!

But mark the Rustic, *haggis-fed*,
The trembling earth resounds his tread,
Clap in his walie nieve a blade,
   He'll make it whissle;
An' legs, an' arms, an' heads will sned,
   Like taps o' thrissle.

Ye Pow'rs wha mak mankind your care,
And dish them out their bill o' fare,
Auld Scotland wants nae skinking ware
   That jaups in luggies;
But, if ye wish her gratefu' prayer,
   Gie her a *Haggis*!

Robert Burns

Fragment I

Roe deer,
    breaking from a thicket

bounding over briars
    between darkening trees

you don't even glance
    at the cause of your doubt

so how can you tell
    what form I take?

What form I take
    I scarcely know myself

adrift in a wood
    in wintertime at dusk

always a deer
    breaking from a thicket

for a while now
    this is how it's been

Kathleen Jamie

27

Nora's Vow

Hear what Highland Nora said, –
'The Earlie's son I will not wed,
Should all the race of nature die,
And none be left but he and I.
For all the gold, for all the gear,
And all the lands both far and near
That ever valour lost or won,
I would not wed the Earlie's son.'

'A Maiden's vows,' old Callum spoke,
'Are lightly made and lightly broke;
The heather on the mountain's height
Begins to bloom in purple light;
The frost-wind soon shall sweep away
That lustre deep from glen and brae;
Yet Nora, ere its bloom be gone,
May blithely wed the Earlie's son.'

'The swan,' she said, 'the lake's clear breast
May barter for the eagle's nest;
The Awe's fierce stream may backward turn,
Ben-Cruaichan fall, and crush Kilchurn;
Our kilted clans, when blood is high,
Before their foes may turn and fly;
But I, were all these marvels done,
Would never wed the Earlie's son.'

Still in the water-lily's shade
Her wonted nest the wild-swan made;
Ben-Cruaichan stands as fast as ever,
Still downward foams the Awe's fierce river;
To shun the clash of foeman's steel
No Highland brogue has turn'd the heel;
But Nora's heart is lost and won,
– She's wedded to the Earlie's son!

Sir Walter Scott

28

The Little White Rose

To John Gawsworth

The rose of all the world is not for me.
I want for my part
Only the little white rose of Scotland
That smells sharp and sweet – and breaks the heart.

Hugh MacDiarmid

January

29

Ceòl san Eaglais

'S toil leam an coithional a fhreagras gu greannach,
dòchas a' dìosgail tro bheathannan doirbhe;
's toil leam còisirean ghuthanna geala,
solas a' lìonadh àiteachan dorcha;
ach is annsa leam an coithional nach seinn ach
  meadhanach –
an salmadair nach buail air na puingean àrda,
an tè a cheileireas os cionn na h-uile,
an t-organaiche a thòisicheas air rann a bharrachd;
oir 's ann an sin a thèid an gaol a dhùshlanachadh,
eadar àilleasachd is dìomhanas is breòiteachd daonna,
's ann an sin ge b' oil leam a nochdas am beannachadh –
am fios nach eil lorg air ceòl nas binne.

Meg Bateman

42

Music in Church

I like a growling congregation,
hope creaking through difficult lives;
I like choirs of bright voices,
light filling dark places;
but best I like indifferent singing –
the soloist who gets the high notes flat,
the warbler who makes herself heard over all,
the organist who embarks on an extra verse;
for here is the greater challenge to love,
amid fastidiousness, vanity, human failing,
here too, appears the greater blessing,
on knowing it sweeter than any singing.

Meg Bateman

30

Physics for the unwary student

1. Imagine that you are trying to balance on the surface of an expanding balloon. List all the different ways in which this resembles reality.

2. Thousands of sub-atomic particles stream through you night and day. Does this account for those peculiar flashes of light you sometimes see?

3. You are trapped in a lift which is plummeting to the ground. Describe what you feel.

4. You are in a spaceship travelling towards a black hole. As you pass the event horizon and become cut off from the rest of the Universe, what do you observe?

5. What happens if you stop believing in gravity? Will you slide off the Earth?

6. What happens if you stop believing?

Pippa Goldschmidt

31

I shall leave tonight from Euston

I shall leave tonight from Euston
By the seven-thirty train,
And from Perth in the early morning
I shall see the hills again.
From the top of Ben Macdhui
I shall watch the gathering storm,
And see the crisp snow lying
At the back of Cairngorm.
I shall feel the mist from Bhrotain
And pass by Lairig Ghru
To look on dark Loch Einich
From the heights of Sgoran Dubh.
From the broken Barns of Bynack
I shall see the sunrise gleam
On the forehead of Ben Rinnes
And Strathspey awake from dream.
And again in the dusk of evening
I shall find once more alone
The dark water of the Green Loch
And the pass beyond Ryvoan.
For tonight I leave from Euston
And leave the world behind;
Who has the hills for a lover
Will find them wondrous kind.

Anon.

February

I

Deliverance

I'm waiting for the star to rise
– a planet maybe

that every evening tangles itself
in the still leafless branches

of the sycamore
framed by your smallest window

where it seems to flutter and tremble
like thon pied wagtail,

mind? trapped in a lobster-creel
on the pier at Elgol.

O fisherman's hand, reach in!
Send us chirruping!

Kathleen Jamie

2

Outwith

'outwith': preposition: outside; beyond. A term
unique to Scotland.

Revising my visa essay,
applying for three more years
here, I read my own scribbled words:

Comparable opportunities for critical study
do not exist outwith Scotland.

Outwith: a term unfamiliar, yet
scrawled in my own hand,
doubtlessly mine, and I wonder:

I came here all rude American brass, all
trash can, fanny pack, Where's the castle?

Then Glasgow rolled itself under my tongue,
a grey marble lolling my mouth open with Os:
Glasgow, Kelvingrove, going to Tesco,

then thistling my speech wi sleekit lisps,
wee packets a crisps,

my lips like the lids
of those glass bottles of sand
I used to collect from every beach:
my mouth a shore holding each grain
that altered the flow of my speech,

my pen flowing 's' into the cursive waves
of 'socialised', 'civilised', 'acclimatised',
answering *Aye!* by accident
then smiling.

I may be from *out*
but I am now *with.*

Katie Ailes

3

Doras-Cuartachaidh

Choisich i mach orm
A-mach air an doras-chuartachaidh
Ach 's eudar gun deach rud air choreigin ceàrr
Air an uidheam,
Oir, a dh' aithghearr
'S ann a thill i gam ionnsaigh.

Rody Gorman

Revolving Door

She walked out on me,
Out through the revolving door
But something or other must have gone wrong
With the mechanism
Because, shortly afterwards,
She came back to me.

Rody Gorman

4

You Might As Well . . .

Small brothers blame you;
Big ones skulk;
Mothers shame you;
Sisters sulk.
Dads won't budge
Unless you shove 'em.
But they're family;
You might as well love 'em.

Lindsay MacRae

5

In the Highlands

In the highlands, in the country places,
Where the old plain men have rosy faces,
And the young fair maidens
Quiet eyes;
Where essential silence cheers and blesses,
And forever in the hill-recesses
Her more lovely music
Broods and dies.

O to mount again where erst I haunted;
Where the old red hills are bird-enchanted,
And the low green meadows
Bright with sward;
And when even dies, the million-tinted,
And the night has come, and planets glinted,
Lo, the valley hollow
Lamp-bestarred!

O to dream, O to awake and wander
There, and with delight to take and render,
Through the trance of silence,
Quiet breath;
Lo! for there, among the flowers and grasses,
Only the mightier movement sounds and passes;
Only winds and rivers,
Life and death.

Robert Louis Stevenson

6

Lochinvar

O, young Lochinvar is come out of the west,
Through all the wide Border his steed was the best;
And save his good broadsword he weapons had none,
He rode all unarmed, and he rode all alone.
So faithful in love, and so dauntless in war,
There never was knight like the young Lochinvar.

He staid not for brake, and he stopped not for stone.
He swam the Eske river where ford there was none;
But ere he alighted at Netherby gate,
The bride had consented, the gallant came late:
For a laggard in love, and a dastard in war,
Was to wed the fair Ellen of brave Lochinvar.

So boldly he entered the Netherby Hall,
Among bride's-men, and kinsmen, and brothers, and all:
Then spoke the bride's father, his hand on his sword,
(For the poor craven bridegroom said never a word,)
'O come ye in peace here, or come ye in war,
Or to dance at our bridal, young Lord Lochinvar?'

'I long wooed your daughter, my suit you denied; –
Love swells like the Solway, but ebbs like its tide –
And now am I come, with this lost love of mine,
To lead but one measure, drink one cup of wine.
There are maidens in Scotland more lovely by far,
That would gladly be bride to the young Lochinvar.'

The bride kissed the goblet: the knight took it up,
He quaffed off the wine, and he threw down the cup.
She looked down to blush, and she looked up to sigh,
With a smile on her lips, and a tear in her eye.
He took her soft hand, ere her mother could bar, –
'Now tread we a measure!' said young Lochinvar.

So stately his form, and so lovely her face,
That never a hall such a galliard did grace;
While her mother did fret, and her father did fume.
And the bridegroom stood dangling his bonnet and plume;
And the bride-maidens whispered "Twere better by far,
To have matched our fair cousin with young Lochinvar.'

One touch to her hand, and one word in her ear,
When they reached the hall-door, and the charger stood near;
So light to the croupe the fair lady he swung,
So light to the saddle before her he sprung!
'She is won! we are gone, over bank, bush, and scaur;
They'll have fleet steeds that follow,' quoth young Lochinvar.

There was mounting 'mong Graemes of the Netherby clan;
Forsters, Fenwicks, and Musgraves, they rode and they ran:
There was racing and chasing on Cannobie Lee,
But the lost bride of Netherby ne'er did they see.
So daring in love, and so dauntless in war,
Have ye e'er heard of gallant like young Lochinvar?

Sir Walter Scott

7

The Bonnie Earl of Moray

Ye Highlands and ye Lawlands,
    Oh! where hae ye been?
They hae slain the Earl of Moray,
    And hae laid him on the green.

Now wae be to thee, Huntly,
    And wherefore did you sae?
I bade you bring him wi' you,
    But forbade you him to slay.

He was a braw gallant,
    And he rid at the ring;
And the bonnie Earl of Moray,
    Oh! he might hae been a king.

He was a braw gallant,
    And he play'd at the ba';
And the bonnie Earl of Moray
    Was the flower amang them a'.

He was a braw gallant,
    And he play'd at the glove;
And the bonnie Earl of Moray,
    Oh! he was the Queen's luve.

Oh! lang will his lady
    Look owre the castle Doune,
Ere she see the Earl of Moray
    Come sounding thro' the toun.

Anon.

8

Alas! Poor Queen

She was skilled in music and the dance
And the old arts of love
At the court of the poisoned rose
And the perfumed glove,
And gave her beautiful hand
To the pale Dauphin
A triple crown to win –
And she loved little dogs
   And parrots
   And red-legged partridges
And the golden fishes of the Duc de Guise
And a pigeon with a blue ruff
She had from Monsieur d'Elboeuf.

Master John Knox was no friend to her;
She spoke him soft and kind,
Her honeyed words were Satan's lure
The unwary soul to bind.
'Good sir, doth a lissome shape
And a comely face
Offend your God His Grace
Whose Wisdom maketh these
Golden fishes of the Duc de Guise?'

She rode through Liddesdale with a song;
'Ye streams sae wondrous strang,
Oh, mak' me a wrack as I come back
But spare me as I gang.'
While a hill-bird cried and cried
Like a spirit lost
By the grey storm-wind tost.

Consider the way she had to go,
Think of the hungry snare,
The net she herself had woven,
Aware or unaware,
Of the dancing feet grown still,
The blinded eyes –
Queens should be cold and wise,
And she loved little things,
　Parrots
　And red-legged partridges
And the golden fishes of the Duc de Guise
And the pigeon with the blue ruff
She had from Monsieur d'Elboeuf.

Marion Angus

9

The Word Party

Loving words clutch crimson roses,
Rude words sniff and pick their noses,
Sly words come dressed up as foxes,
Short words stand on cardboard boxes,
Common words tell jokes and gabble,
Complicated words play Scrabble,
Swear words stamp around and shout,
Hard words stare each other out,
Foreign words look lost and shrug,
Careless words trip on the rug,
Long words slouch with stooping shoulders,
Code words carry secret folders,
Silly words flick rubber bands,
Hyphenated words hold hands,
Strong words show off, bending metal,
Sweet words call each other 'petal',
Small words yawn and suck their thumbs
Till at last the morning comes.
Kind words give out farewell posies . . .

Snap! The dictionary closes.

Richard Edwards

10

What I Wanted

was such a plump, bountiful
landscape of snow, more
than I'd ever dared wish for.
That was back when we had
proper winters, long ago,
when lawns and driveways
vanished: there were
no boundaries. Fences, walls,
gardens and homes dropped off
the edge of the world.
There was a muffled
silence each night when
darkness married with snow
to wake me from dreams
that began and ended
with the snow. I was hidden
from view behind a tree
whose branches were
perilously bent and laden
with snow, watching
a dark figure disappear;
then I would slip out fearlessly,
sure-footed and fleet,

with my magnifying glass
and pocket torch to follow
the tracks that led off as far
as a child's eye could see,
and then a little further.

Tracey Herd

11

The River of Life

The more we live, more brief appear
  Our life's succeeding stages:
A day to childhood seems a year,
  And years like passing ages.

The gladsome current of our youth,
  Ere passion yet disorders,
Steals lingering like a river smooth
  Along its grassy borders.

But as the careworn cheek grows wan,
  And sorrow's shafts fly thicker,
Ye Stars, that measure life to man,
  Why seem your courses quicker?

When joys have lost their bloom and breath
  And life itself is vapid,
Why, as we reach the Falls of Death,
  Feel we its tide more rapid?

It may be strange — yet who would change
  Time's course to slower speeding,
When one by one our friends have gone
  And left our bosoms bleeding?

Heaven gives our years of fading strength
    Indemnifying fleetness;
And those of youth, a seeming length,
    Proportion'd to their sweetness.

Thomas Campbell

12

Scotland

It requires great love of it deeply to read
The configuration of a land,
Gradually grow conscious of fine shadings,
Of great meanings in slight symbols,
Hear at last the great voice that speaks softly,
See the swell and fall upon the flank
Of a statue carved out in a whole country's marble,
Be like Spring, like a hand in a window
Moving New and Old things carefully to and fro,
Moving a fraction of flower here,
Placing an inch of air there,
And without breaking anything.
So I have gathered unto myself
All the loose ends of Scotland,
And by naming them and accepting them,
Loving them and identifying myself with them,
Attempt to express the whole.

Hugh MacDiarmid

13

Flight Radar

From the top of the Shard the view unfolds
down the Thames to the sea, the city laid
by a trick of sight vertically in front of me.
At London Bridge Station, trains slide in

and out in a long slow dance. It is not
by chance that I am here, not looking down
but up to where you are on Flight 199,
coming in to land. I have learned to track you

on my mobile phone. However far you go,
I have the app that uses the radar to trace
your path. There you are now, circling down
around this spire where I stand, my face reflected

over your pulse in the glass. You cannot see.
You have no radar for me, no app to make you
look back or down to where I am lifting my hand.
Darling, I will track your flight till it is a dot

that turns and banks and falls out of sight, looking
into the space where you were. Fingers frozen
on the tiny keys, I will stay where I am
in the dying light, the screen still live in my palm.

Imtiaz Dharker

14

The Confirmation

Yes, yours, my love, is the right human face.
I in my mind had waited for this long,
Seeing the false and searching for the true,
Then found you as a traveller finds a place
Of welcome suddenly amid the wrong
Valleys and rocks and twisting roads. But you,
What shall I call you? A fountain in a waste,
A well of water in a country dry,
Or anything that's honest and good, an eye
That makes the whole world bright. Your open heart,
Simple with giving, gives the primal deed,
The first good world, the blossom, the blowing seed,
The hearth, the steadfast land, the wandering sea,
Not beautiful or rare in every part,
But like yourself, as they were meant to be.

Edwin Muir

15

A Red, Red Rose

O my luve's like a red, red rose,
That's newly sprung in June:
O my luve's like the melodie
That's sweetly play'd in tune.

As fair art thou, my bonny lass,
So deep in luve am I;
And I will luve thee still, my dear,
Till a' the seas gang dry.

Till a' the seas gang dry, my dear,
And the rocks melt wi' the sun
O I will luve thee still, my dear,
While the sands o' life shall run:

And fare thee weel, my only luve!
And fare thee weel a while!
And I will come again, my luve,
Though it were ten thousand mile.

Robert Burns

16

Semaphore

An e na brataich cheàrr a tha mi 'cur a-mach
's nach tuig thu an teachdaireachd
a tha 'gluasad anns a' ghaoth?
An e am pàtaran a tha ceàrr
neo na dathan
's gu bheil thusa 'leughadh rud nach eil mi 'g ràdh?
Neo a bheil thu ri cleas Nelson:
a' toirt a' chreids nach fhaic thu
gus nach bi agad
ri freagairt a thoirt dhomh?

Anne Frater

Semaphore

Is it because I'm hanging out the wrong flags
that you can't read the message
that's moving in the wind?
Are the patterns wrong
or the colours
making you read it all wrong?
Or are you, like Nelson,
pretending you can't see
so you don't have to give me
an answer?

Anne Frater

17

Consolation

Though he, that ever kind and true,
Kept stoutly step by step with you,
Your whole long gusty lifetime through,
      Be gone awhile before,
Be now a moment gone before,
Yet, doubt not, soon the seasons shall restore
      Your friend to you.

He has but turned a corner – still
He pushes on with right good will,
Through mire and marsh, by heugh and hill,
      That self-same arduous way –
That self-same upland, hopeful way
That you and he through many a doubtful day
      Attempted still.

He is not dead, this friend – not dead,
But in the path we mortals tread
Got some few trifling steps ahead
      And nearer to the end;
So that you too, once past the bend,
Shall meet again, as face to face, this friend
      You fancy dead.

Push gaily on, strong heart! The while
You travel forward mile by mile,
He loiters with a backward smile
    Till you can overtake,
And strains his eyes to search his wake,
Or whistling, as he sees you through the brake,
    Waits on a stile.

Robert Louis Stevenson

18

The Wonderfu' Wean

Our wean's the most wonderfu' wean e'er I saw,
It would tak' me a lang summer day to tell a'
His pranks, frae the morning till night shuts his e'e,
When he sleeps like a peerie, 'tween father and me.
For in his quiet turns, siccan questions he'll speir:
How the moon can stick up in the sky that's sae clear?
What gars the wind blaw? and wharfrae comes the rain?
He's a perfect divert: he's a wonderfu' wean!

Or wha was the first body's father? and wha
Made the very first snaw-shower that ever did fa'?
And wha made the first bird that sang on a tree?
And the water that sooms a' the ships on the sea? –
But after I've tell't him as weel as I ken,
Again he begins wi' his 'Wha?' and his 'When?'
And he looks aye sae watchfu' the while I explain, –
He's as auld as the hills – he's an auld-farrant wean.

And folk wha ha'e skill o' the lumps on the head,
Hint there's mae ways than toiling o' winning ane's bread;
How he'll be a rich man, and ha'e men to work for him,
Wi' a kyte like a bailie's, shug-shugging afore him,
Wi' a face like the moon, sober, sonsy, and douce,
And a back, for its breadth, like the side o' a house.
'Tweel I'm unco tae'en up wi't, they mak' a' sae plain, –
He's just a town's talk – he's a by-ord'nar wean!

I ne'er can forget sic a laugh as I gat,
When I saw him put on his father's waistcoat and hat;
Then the lang-leggit boots gaed sae far owre his knees,
The tap loops wi' his fingers he grippit wi' ease,
Then he march'd thro' the house, he march'd but,
  he march'd ben,
That I leugh clean outright, for I couldna contain,
He was sic a conceit – sic an ancient-like wean.

But 'mid a' his daffin' sic kindness he shows,
That he's dear to my heart as the dew to the rose;
And the unclouded hinnie-beam aye in his e'e,
Mak's him every day dearer and dearer to me.
Though fortune be saucy, and dorty, and dour,
And glooms through her fingers, like hills through a shower,
When bodies hae got ae bit bairn o' their ain,
How he cheers up their hearts, – he's the wonderfu' wean.

William Miller

19

Untitled

I once heard a river as a car,
hovered on a kerb to let the breeze pass.

Traffic is each walker's indrawn breath.
Cyclists make the darkness move nonstop.

I walk on my ears,
the road changing shape as I eavesdrop.

Nuala Watt

20

Fragment 2

Imagine we could begin
all over again; begin

afresh, like this February
dawn light, coaxing

from the Scots pines
their red ochre, burnt-earth glow.

All over again. South
– facing mountainsides, balcony

above balcony of pines – imagine
we could mend

whatever we heard fracture:
splintering of wood, a bird's

cry over still water, a sound
only reaching us now

Kathleen Jamie

21

The Auntie with a Kiss Like a Heat-Seeking Missile

Auntie Enid loves to kiss
Seldom does she ever miss.

Lindsay MacRae

22

The Laird o' Cockpen

The Laird o' Cockpen, he's proud an' he's freat,
His mind is ta'en up wi' the things o' the state;
He wanted a wife his braw house to keep,
But favour wi' wooin' was fashious to seek.

Doun by the dyke-side a lady did dwell,
At his table-head he thought she'd look well;
M'Cleish's ae daughter o' Claverse-ha Lee,
A penniless lass wi' a lang pedigree.

His wig was well pouther'd, and as guid as new,
His waistcoat was white, his coat it was blue;
He put on a ring, a sword, and cock'd hat
And wha could refuse the laird wi' a' that?

He took the grey mare, and rade cannilie,
And rapp'd at the yett o' Claverse-ha Lee:
'Gae tell Mistress Jean to come speedily ben,
She's wanted to speak to the laird o' Cockpen.'

Mistress Jean was makin' the elder-flower wine:
'And what brings the laird at sic a like time?'
She put off her apron and on her silk gown,
Her mutch wi' red ribbons, and gaed awa'-doun.

And when she cam' ben, he bowed fu' low,
And what was his errand he soon let her know;
Amazed was the laird when the lady said 'Na';
And wi' a laigh curtsie she turned awa'.

Dumfounder'd he was, nae sigh did he gie,
He mounted his mare and he rade cannilie;
And often he thought, as he gaed thro' the glen,
She's daft to refuse the laird o' Cockpen.

Carolina Oliphant, Lady Nairne

23

You've got fifteen seconds in which to

You've got fifteen seconds in which to achieve enlightenment, pal.

Peter McCarey

24

Anemones

Anemones, they say, are out
    By sheltered woodland streams,
With budding branches all about
    Where Spring-time sunshine gleams;

Such are the haunts they love, but I
    With swift remembrance see
Anemones beneath a sky
    Of cold austerity –

Pale flowers too faint for winds so chill
    And with too fair a name –
That day I lingered on a hill
    For one who never came.

Marion Angus

25

Orbit of Three

Planets and stars understand
the luxury of love creating
me from my own materials
like God breathing flowers
from the seeded dust. As
abundant blue earth depends
on the sun, I am to you. You
water me. Eye-light leapt the
red boundaries of blood, stain –
glassed my heart; turned the
deaf *thud thud* counting life's
hurrying hours into drums,
duets, urging me on, on.

And we have made a moon,
out of nothing, like magicians
learning God's best trick.

Gillian Ferguson

26

Mountain Burn

I am the mountain burn. I go
Where only hill-folk know;
Pitter-patter, splash and spatter,
Goblin laughter, elfin chatter!
I am a chain of silver under the moon;
A spell that breaks too soon;
Lost voices chuckling across the peat.
Or faery feet
Echoing where the dancing harebells blow.

The silent places know me. Trees,
Stately and cool,
Gaze at their green reflections where I flow
Into some shadowy pool.
I am a ribbon of light,
A flash of blinding-white
Foam where the pale sun lingers
Over the heathery waste.
And still my long green fingers
Probe with a surgeon's skill the perilous grey
Slopes of the ferny gorge to carve away
Granite and stone and bleached bone
To suit my changeling taste.
I am brilliant as the stars, and timeless;
Sad as the Earth, and strong
As mortal love. And through the long
Enchanted hours of sun and showers

I charm the hills with endless, rhymeless
Cadences of song.
And the dry reeds and rushes
Tremble and sigh, quiver and shake,
When the night wind hushes
With lullaby
The dreams that die, the hearts that break —
And only I am left awake . . .

Brenda G. Macrow

27

The Tay Moses

What can I fashion
for you but a woven
creel of river-
rashes, a golden
oriole's nest, my gift
wrought from the Firth –

and choose my tide: either
the flow, when, watertight
you'll drift to the uplands –
my favourite hills; held safe
in eddies, where salmon, wisdom
and guts withered in spawn,
rest between moves – that
slither of body as you were born –

or the ebb, when the water
will birl you to snag
on reeds, the river-
pilot leaning over the side:
'Name o God!' and you'll change hands:
tractor-man, grieve, farm-wife
who takes you into her
competent arms

even as I drive, slamming
the car's gears,
spitting gravel on tracks
down between berry-fields,
engine still racing, the door wide
as I run toward her, crying
LEAVE HIM! Please,
it's okay, he's mine.

Kathleen Jamie

28

Scotland My Lover

There are mountains that are more to me than men,
There are rivers that are more to me than love,
There's a rock where my soul takes cover.
Wild winds on a maddened world have driven,
Lifted me up to the bare hills above,
      Scotland, my Lover.

Here is a lover who will never change.
In storm and stillness, every lightning mood,
New ways of loving I'll discover,
A living sureness nothing can estrange.
Your grief and joy will be my daily food,
      Scotland, my Lover.

Ours is the love of lovers born to belong,
Our hearts sing the same music, beat as one.
Our glass of 'the water of life' brims over,
Our thrice-rich, flowering native song,
Prodigal and gay. And, when my song is done,
      I'll lie with you, my Lover.

Clear northern skies lit childhood's innocence.
The day's darg over, dew under my feet, bare
on the cool grass, stars blaze and hover.
O still make love with me, far from the decadence
of this dire century, of love's despair,
     Scotland, my Jewel, my Lover.

Nannie Katharin Wells

Gazetteer

Stromeferry
(no ferry)

Muir of Ord
(no ford)

Carrbridge
(no bridge)

Mitherwell
(no well)

Ullapool
(no pool)

Dingwall (no wall)
Redpoint (no point at all)

Kirkintilloch
(no loch)

Stornoway
(no way)

Portree
(no tree)

Aviemore
(no more)

Gourock
(no rock)

Knockando
(do).

Rody Gorman

March

I

Kiss

For want of a mountain a primrose was lost,
For want of a primrose a love song was lost,
For want of a love song a sly kiss was lost,
And that was the thing that mattered most,
Yes, that was the thing that mattered most.

Robert Crawford

2

Farm Sale

Everything is numbered and must go
so he sits at the back of the shed
while the crowd pick over the final lots.

He lays his cap flat on his knee,
slowly stretches a stiff finger
to find the faded cross hatch flecks

tracing each tweed field on his bunnet,
whispering their sweet names to himself,
walking the boundaries of his lost world.

Jim Carruth

3

I Opened a Book

I opened a book and in I strode.
Now nobody can find me.
I've left my chair, my house, my road,
My town and my world behind me.

I'm wearing the cloak, I've slipped on the ring,
I've swallowed the magic potion.
I've fought with a dragon, dined with a king
And dived in a bottomless ocean.

I opened a book and made some friends.
I shared their tears and laughter
And followed their road with its bumps and bends
To the happily ever after.

I finished my book and out I came.
The cloak can no longer hide me.
My chair and my house are just the same,
But I have a book inside me.

Julia Donaldson

4

On a Cat, Ageing

He blinks upon the hearth-rug,
And yawns in deep content,
Accepting all the comforts
That Providence has sent.

Louder he purrs and louder,
In one glad hymn of praise
For all the night's adventures,
For quiet restful days.

Life will go on forever,
With all that cat can wish;
Warmth and the glad procession
Of fish and milk and fish.

Only – the thought disturbs him –
He's noticed once or twice,
The times are somehow breeding
A nimbler race of mice.

Sir Alexander Gray

5

Magpie

One is sorrow, two is mirth,
three a wedding, four a birth,
five heaven, six hell,
seven's the de'il's ain sel!

Anon.

6

Doctor Wha

Wha's Doctor Wha? Wha better kens nor he
that jouks the yetts and rides the birlin wheels
o time and space, shape-shiftin as he reels
through endless versions o reality?
Bit dis he ken himsel? Weel, mibbe sae,
yet wha's tae ken gin aw that's kent by Wha
maks mair or less or better sense ava
nor whit we ithers ken, or think we dae?
The universe is fou o parallels:
wha's like us? Hunners? Thoosans? We oorsels
micht be mere glisks o life-forms yet tae be.
Whit's real? Whaur's here? When's noo? Wha's quick or deid?
Wha's jist a thoctie in anither's heid?
Wha's Doctor Wha? Wha better kens nor s/he?

James Robertson

7

Eòin

Rounded,
you begin life's voyage.

Somewhere,
where God breathed life into the very dust,

you were linked with a moment, a woman, a page, a poem.

Angus Peter Campbell

8

The Gowk

I see the gowk,
An the gowk sees me
Atween the berry buss
An the aipple tree.

Anon.

9

Slate

There is no beginning. We saw Lewis
laid down, when there was not much but thunder
and volcanic fires; watched long seas plunder
faults; laughed as Staffa cooled. Drumlins blue as
bruises were grated off like nutmegs; bens, and
a great glen, gave a rough back we like
to think the ages must streak, surely strike,
seldom stroke, but raised and shaken, with tens
of thousands of rains, blizzards, sea-poundings
shouldered off into night and memory.
Memory of men! That was to come. Great
in their empty hunger these surroundings
threw walls to the sky, the sorry glory
of a rainbow. Their heels kicked flint, chalk, slate.

Edwin Morgan

10

Ae Fond Kiss

Ae fond kiss, and then we sever;
Ae fareweel, alas, for ever!
Deep in heart-wrung tears I'll pledge thee,
Warring sighs and groans I'll wage thee.
Who shall say that Fortune grieves him,
While the star of hope she leaves him?
Me, nae cheerfu' twinkle lights me;
Dark despair around benights me.

I'll ne'er blame my partial fancy:
Naething could resist my Nancy!
But to see her was to love her,
Love but her, and love for ever.
Had we never lov'd sae kindly,
Had we never lov'd sae blindly,
Never met – or never parted –
We had ne'er been broken-hearted.
Fare-thee-weel, thou first and fairest!
Fare-thee-weel, thou best and dearest!
Thine be ilka joy and treasure,
Peace, enjoyment, love and pleasure!
Ae fond kiss, and then we sever!
Ae fareweel, alas, for ever!
Deep in heart-wrung tears I'll pledge thee,
Warring sighs and groans I'll wage thee.

Robert Burns

11

Hop and Hope

every day
more bluebells
more yellow poppies

the pair of dunnocks
and the blackbird
must be feeding young
they can't get enough
breadcrumbs

they hop about
the cut grass
hoping for
beasties

Hamish Whyte

12

Small

i.m. Roanne Dods

It's always the small that
gets you, a wee act
of kindness, the tiniest detail,
a stranger's caress,
your heart, the way you react
when faced with the trials.
The gift of a bluebell, an embrace,
Oh – the yellow gorse,
the small brown foals,
the crows lined up
from the train window.
Beauty, inches close to sorrow.

Jackie Kay

13

The Season of Youth

Rejoice, mortal man, in the noon of thy prime!
Ere thy brow shall be traced by the ploughshare of time,
Ere the twilight of age shall encompass thy way,
And thou droop'st, like the flowers, to thy rest in the clay.

Let the banquet be spread, let the wine-cup go round,
Let the joy-dance be wove, let the timbrels resound,
While the spring-tide of life in thy bosom is high,
And thy spirit is light as a lark in the sky.

Let the wife of thy love, like the sun of thy day,
Throw a radiance of joy o'er thy pilgrimage way –
Ere the shadows of grief come, like night, from the west,
And thou weep'st o'er the flower that expired on thy breast.

Rejoice, mortal man, in the noon of thy prime!
But muse on the power and the progress of time;
For thy life shall depart with the joy it hath given,
And a judgement of justice awaits thee in heaven.

William Knox

14

Love

And said I that my limbs were old,
And said I that my blood was cold,
And that my kindly fire was fled,
And my poor withered heart was dead,
    And that I might not sing of love? –
How could I to the dearest theme,
That ever warmed a minstrel's dream,
    So foul, so false a recreant prove!
How could I name love's very name,
Nor wake my heart to notes of flame!

In peace, Love tunes the shepherd's reed;
In war, he mounts the warrior's steed;
In halls, in gay attire is seen;
In hamlets, dances on the green,
Love rules the court, the camp, the grove,
And men below, and saints above;
For love is heaven, and heaven is love.

Sir Walter Scott

15

Spring-Song

The air was full of sun and birds,
  The fresh air sparkled clearly.
Remembrance wakened in my heart
  And I knew I loved her dearly.

The fallows and the leafless trees
  And all my spirit tingled.
My earliest thought of love, and spring's
  First puff of perfume mingled.

In my still heart, the thoughts awoke
  Came bone by bone together –
Say, birds and sun and spring, is love
  A mere affair of weather?

Robert Louis Stevenson

16

Eclipse

The city spills light. But the moon,
in a clear sky, holds its own,
diaphanous and vulnerable,
a sliver of rime – till
full circle again,
the eclipse might never have been.
Tempting when all returns to normal
to forget what made us marvel,
or wonder if it really happened.
Back in bed, I slip a hand
gently across, touch your shoulder,
just to make sure you are still there.

Stewart Conn

17

March Weather

Wind in pines
wind on water
wind in rushes
wind on feather

Sun in leaves
sun on loch
sun in reeds
sun on duck

Rain in trees
rain on river
rain in moss
rain on eider

All one morning
all together
in an hour
March weather

Tessa Ransford

18

The Banks o' Doon

Ye banks and braes o' bonnie Doon
    How can ye bloom sae fair!
How can ye chant, ye little birds,
    And I sae fu' o' care!

Thou'll break my heart, thou bonnie bird
    That sings upon the bough;
Thou minds me o' the happy days
    When my fause Luve was true.

Thou'll break my heart, thou bonnie bird
    That sings beside thy mate;
For sae I sat, and sae I sang,
    And wist na o' my fate.

Aft hae I roved by bonnie Doon
    To see the woodbine twine,
And ilka bird sang o' its love;
    And sae did I o' mine.

Wi' lightsome heart I pu'd a rose,
    Frae aff its thorny tree;
And my fause luver staw the rose,
    But left the thorn wi' me.

Robert Burns

19

Grandpa's Soup

No one makes soup like my Grandpa's,
with its diced carrots the perfect size
and its diced potatoes the perfect size
and its wee soft bits –
what are their names?
and its big bit of hough,
which rhymes with loch, floating
like a rich island in the middle of the soup sea.

I say, Grandpa, Grandpa your soup is the best
    soup in the whole world.
And Grandpa says, Och,
which rhymes with hough and loch,
Och, don't be daft,
because he's shy about his soup, my Grandpa.
He knows I will grow up and pine for it.
I will fall ill and desperately need it.
I will long for it my whole life after he is gone.
Every soup will become sad and wrong after he is gone.
He knows when I'm older I will avoid soup altogether.
Oh Grandpa, Grandpa, why is your soup so glorious? I say
tucking into my fourth bowl in a day.

Barley! That's the name of the wee soft bits.
Barley.

Jackie Kay

20

from To His Mistress

My dear and only Love, I pray
    This noble World of thee,
Be govern'd by no other Sway
    But purest Monarchie.
For if Confusion have a Part,
    Which vertuous Souls abhore,
And hold a Synod in thy Heart,
    I'll never love thee more.

Like Alexander I will reign,
    And I will reign alone,
My Thoughts shall evermore disdain
    A Rival on my Throne.
He either fears his Fate too much,
    Or his Deserts are small,
That puts it not unto the Touch,
    To win or lose it all . . .

But if thou wilt be constant then,
    And faithful of thy Word,
I'll make thee glorious by my Pen,
    And famous by my Sword.
I'll serve thee in such noble Ways
    Was never heard before:
I'll crown and deck thee all with Bays,
    And love thee evermore.

James Graham,
Marquess of Montrose

21

All for Love

O talk not to me of a name great in story;
The days of our youth are the days of our glory;
And the myrtle and ivy of sweet two-and-twenty
Are worth all your laurels, though ever so plenty.

What are garlands and crowns to the brow that is wrinkled?
'Tis but as a dead flower with May-dew besprinkled:
Then away with all such from the head that is hoary –
What care I for the wreaths that can only give glory?

O Fame! – if I e'er took delight in thy praises,
'Twas less for the sake of thy high-sounding phrases,
Than to see the bright eyes of the dear one discover
She thought that I was not unworthy to love her.

There chiefly I sought thee, there only I found thee;
Her glance was the best of the rays that surround thee;
When it sparkled o'er aught that was bright in my story,
I knew it was love, and I felt it was glory.

George Gordon, Lord Byron

22

The Blue Jacket

When there comes a flower to the stingless nettle,
    To the hazel bushes, bees,
I think I can see my little sister
    Rocking herself by the hazel trees.

Rocking her arms for very pleasure
    That every leaf so sweet can smell,
And that she has on her the warm blue jacket
    Of mine, she liked so well.

Oh to win near you, little sister!
    To hear your soft lips say –
'I'll never tak' up wi' lads or lovers,
    But a baby I maun hae.

'A baby in a cradle rocking,
    Like a nut, in a hazel shell,
And a new blue jacket, like this o' Annie's,
    It sets me aye sae well.'

Marion Angus

23

Sticks an stanes

Sticks an stanes
Will brak ma banes,
But names will never hurt me.
Whan A'm deid,
An in ma grave,
Ye'll be sorry fir whit ye ca'd me.

Anon.

24

Jean

Of a' the airts the wind can blaw
 I dearly like the West,
For there the bonnie lassie lives,
 The lassie I lo'e best:
There wild woods grow, and rivers row,
 And mony a hill between;
But day and night my fancy's flight
 Is ever wi' my Jean.

I see her in the dewy flowers,
 I see her sweet and fair:
I hear her in the tunefu' birds,
 I hear her charm the air:
There's not a bonnie flower that springs
 By fountain, shaw, or green,
There's not a bonnie bird that sings
 But minds me o' my Jean.

O blaw ye westlin winds, blaw saft
 Amang the leafy trees;
Wi' balmy gale, frae hill and dale
 Bring hame the laden bees;
And bring the lassie back to me
 That's ay sae neat and clean;
Ae smile o' her wad banish care,
 Sae charming is my Jean.

What sighs and vows amang the knowes
  Hae pass'd atween us twa!
How fond to meet, how wae to part
  That night she gaed awa!
The Powers aboon can only ken,
  To whom the heart is seen,
That nane can be sae dear to me
  As my sweet lovely Jean!

Robert Burns

25

A Minute to Midnight

A minute to midnight
and all is still.

For example, these are things that are still:
ornaments, coins, lamp-posts,
the cooker, Major Clark's Home for old folk
(just opposite our house, which is also still),
the newsagent's, a hut, soap, tractors,
freshly ironed trousers draped over the chair.

A minute to midnight
and all is still
except for the things that are moving.

Like, for example,
rivers, clouds, leaves, flags,
creaky windmills, lungs, birds' feathers,
digital clocks, grass, the wind,
non-sleeping animals (especially wolves),
planet Earth, the moon, satellites in space,
toenails (well they grow, don't they),
videos that are set to record
programmes in the middle of the night,
washing lines,
mobiles above babies' cots –
and babies' eyelids, they always flicker.

John Rice

26

Grandmother

carries the guid Scots tongue in her heid
all the way to London

where it becomes like the kitchen china
worn and cracked with use

kept in the press with the girdle and the spurtle,
the ashet and the jeelie pan.

The good china of English
is what you bring out for visitors:

kept in the credenza
with the key in its lock.

Lift it carefully onto the silver-plated tray.
Remember which language

you're speaking in. Dinnae –
Dinnae forget.

Elizabeth Burns

Spring

But still I must remember how the sound
Of waters echoed in my ear all night,
How fitfully I slumbered, waked, and found
The singing burns, the cataracts, the might

Of tumults drunken with the melting snow,
Filling the starry darkness with their joy;
And heard the singing stars, that paused to know
What shout was that? what rapture, 'Spring, ahoy!'

Nan Shepherd

28

Sounds Like

without any fuss
the cherry blossom is back
the bees are humming

      in the peony
      the bee cannae be ony
      thing bit hummle

two magpies silent
in the cherry tree the leaves
drop they clatter off

Hamish Whyte

29

Escape at Bedtime

The lights from the parlour and kitchen shone out
  Through the blinds and the windows and bars;
And high overhead and all moving about,
  There were thousands of millions of stars.

There ne'er were such thousands of leaves on a tree,
  Nor of people in church or the Park,
As the crowds of the stars that looked down upon me,
  And that glittered and winked in the dark.

The Dog, and the Plough, and the Hunter, and all,
  And the star of the sailor, and Mars,
These shone in the sky, and the pail by the wall
  Would be half full of water and stars.

They saw me at last, and they chased me with cries,
  And they soon had me packed into bed;
But the glory kept shining and bright in my eyes,
  And the stars going round in my head.

Robert Louis Stevenson

30

Dreamscape at Bedtime

The lichts frae the harbour and ferries shone oot
    frae the cafes, amusements and bars;
whilst high owreheid a' movin' aboot
    there were thoosans an' millions o' stars.

The beams frae the lichthoose sprayed owre the sea,
    a ship had white een lik' a shark.
An' the pattern o' planets poored their pure licht on me
    as they glimmered and winked in the dark.

The Great Bear and Venus, the Plough and the moon
    were torches that lit up the nicht;
and the waater was speckled lik' an auld table spoon
    reflectin' a cauld, siller licht.

I woke up at last fu' o' wonder and sighs
    to find I wis waarm in ma bed;
but the marvel kept spinnin' and clear in ma een,
    an' the stars going roon' in ma head.

John Rice

31

Letter from a Spring Garden

'Form is the ultimate gift that love can offer.'
– Adrienne Rich, 'At a Bach Concert'

I love when the cherry blossom's
just out
it usually lasts around
a week

and I love when the wind blows it
about
like snowflakes, the white against
the green.

You're not here but I can tell you all
about
the fragile purity of the blossom,
its fall.

Hamish Whyte

April

I

The Loch Ness Monster's Song

Sssnnnwhufffll?
Hnwhuffl hhnnwfl hnfl hfl?
Gdroblboblhobngbl gbl gl g g g g glbgl.
Drublhaflablhaflubhafgabhaflhafl fl fl —
gm grawwwww grf grawf awfgm graw gm.
Hovoplodok — doplodovok — plovodokot-doplodokosh?
Splgraw fok fok splgrafhatchgabrlgabrl fok splfok!
Zgra kra gka fok!
Grof grawff gahf?
Gombl mbl bl —
blm plm,
blm plm,
blm plm,
blp.

Edwin Morgan

2

The Beach

Now this big westerly's
blown itself out,
let's drive to the storm beach.

A few brave souls
will be there already,
eyeing the driftwood,

the heaps of frayed
blue polyprop rope,
cut loose, thrown back at us –

What a species –
still working the same
curved bay, all of us

hoping for the marvellous,
all hankering for a changed life.

Kathleen Jamie

3

Charlie is my Darling

'Twas on a Monday morning,
  Right early in the year,
When Charlie came to our town
  The young Chevalier.

Charlie is my darling, my darling, my darling,
Charlie is my darling, the young Chevalier.

As he cam' marchin' up the street,
  The pipes played loud and clear.
And a' the folk cam' rinnin' out
  To meet the Chevalier.

Charlie is my darling, my darling, my darling,
Charlie is my darling, the young Chevalier.

Wi' highland bonnets on their heads
  And claymores bright and clear,
They cam' to fight for Scotland's right
  And the young Chevalier.

Charlie is my darling, my darling, my darling,
Charlie is my darling, the young Chevalier.

They've left their bonnie highland hills,
   Their wives and bairnies dear,
To draw the sword for Scotland's lord,
   The young Chevalier.

Charlie is my darling, my darling, my darling,
Charlie is my darling, the young Chevalier.

Oh, there were many beating hearts,
   And mony a hope and fear,
And mony were the pray'rs put up,
   For the young Chevalier.

Charlie is my darling, my darling, my darling,
Charlie is my darling, the young Chevalier.

                      Carolina Oliphant, Lady Nairne

4

Streams

When we went to the grammar school
the teacher said,
'You A-stream girls
will go out in the world
and be doctors and lawyers.
You C-stream girls
will go out into the world
and be typists and mothers.'

But when we left
(tossing our hats in the air),
beyond the school borders,
the streams overflowed
and the dams broke
with the water hoarded
in our hearts
and all the girls flowed
out into the world
in alphabetical disorder.

Diana Hendry

5

My mum's sari

I love my mother's sari on the washing line
Flapping like a giant flag, which I pretend is mine.

I love its silky softness when it's folded to a square
Which I can roll into a ball and pretend it isn't there.

I love to hold its free bit that swings over mum's back
And wrap it round my shoulders, like a potato in a sack.

I love the pleats that fall in shape and spread out like a fan
Where my kid brother crouches and says 'catch me if you can.'

I love to wash my dirty hands at the kitchen sink
And wipe them on mum's sari before she can even blink.

But when she takes her *anchal* and ties it round her waist
I know it's time for battle and a quick escape is best!

Bashabi Fraser

The 'anchal' is the free bit at the end of the sari that is slung over the shoulder.

6

Judith

Judith, why are you kneeling on the lawn
With your ear against that little weed? What are you
    listening for?
Hush, says Judith, go away and leave me,
I'm waiting for this dandelion to roar.

Judith, why are you sitting in the wood
With your eyes fixed on your wristwatch? Do you want to
    know the time?
Hush, says Judith, go away and leave me,
I want to hear the bluebells when they chime.

Judith, why are you standing by that tree
With your handkerchief out ready? Come inside and go to
    sleep.
Hush, says Judith, go away and leave me,
I'm waiting for this willow tree to weep.

Judith, why are you lying in your bed
With some hay stalks in your left hand and some oatflakes in
    your right?
Hush, says Judith, go away and leave me,
A nightmare may come visiting tonight.

Richard Edwards

A St Kilda Lament

It was no crew of landsmen
Crossed the ferry on Wednesday:
'Tis tidings of disaster if you live not.

What has kept you so long from me?
Are the high sea and the sudden wind catching you,
So that you could not at once give her sail?

'Tis a profitless journey
That took the noble men away,
To take our one son from me and from Donald.

My son and my three brothers are gone,
And the one son of my mother's sister,
And, sorest tale, that will come or has come, my husband.

What has set me to draw ashes
And to take a spell at digging
Is that the men are away with no word of their living.

I am left without fun or merriment
Sitting on the floor of the glen;
My eyes are wet, oft are tears on them.

Anon.

8

Desk

It was stuffy in the classroom.
He put his hand inside his desk,
Feeling for a pencil. It was cool in there,
He let his hand swing aimlessly around.
The space within seemed vast, and when
He reached in further he found
Nothing, could feel no books, no ruler.
His hand floated as if in a bath of shadows,
Airy and refreshing, not at all
The same place that the rest of him was in.

He put both hands in, let them drift
Deeper, this way and that. It was more than empty,
The inside had no sides. His hands
Never reappeared through some unexpected hole.
He lifted the lid quietly a little more. A waft
Of soft air cooled his face, the same
As on summer nights or under leafy trees.

He bent his head down to the gap. He looked inside.
Dark as deep water, deep as a clear night sky.
He smiled. He put his head inside.
'What are you doing?' asked the teacher. But he didn't hear.
He slid his shoulders in, and then
Before anyone could reach to stop him,
He bent from the waist, kicking his chair back,
And with a muffled cry of pleasure
Dived. For a split second,
As the room filled with fresh air,
We watched his legs slide slowly down into the desk
And disappear. And then the lid fell back,
Shut, with a soft thud.

Dave Calder

9

The Stags

This is the multitude, the beasts
you wanted to show me, drawing me
upstream, all morning up through wind-
scoured heather to the hillcrest.
Below us, in the next glen, is the grave
calm brotherhood, descended
out of winter, out of hunger, kneeling
like the signatories of a covenant;
their weighty, antique-polished antlers
rising above the vegetation
like masts in a harbour, or city spires.
We lie close together, and though the wind
whips away our man-and-woman smell, every
stag-face seems to look toward us, toward,
but not to us: we're held, and hold them,
in civil regard. I suspect you'd
hoped to impress me, to lift to my sight
our shared country, lead me deeper
into what you know, but loath
to cause fear you're already moving
quietly away, sure I'll go with you,
as I would now, almost anywhere.

Kathleen Jamie

10

The Tree

The heart is a tree for love:
And is a flowery tree
When in its shade the dove
Sings and is free.

Make but your heart a cage,
To hold what you desire,
And song is turned to rage;
Blossom to brier.

William Soutar

II

My Voysey Wall-Paper

I have two gardens for my ease,
Where skies are warm and flowers please;
With skilful mastery each designed
Is fair and perfect of its kind.
In one the tulips every year
Flame April out and disappear;
And roses red that garland June
Are worn but for a summer's noon.
It is a garden, flower and leaf,
Where lovely things are very brief.

Upon a wall my other grows,
And changes not for heat or snows.
Its tulips do not flaunt and die,
But, dreaming, watch the spring go by.
In pensive grey, like musing nuns,
They hold no commerce with the suns.
There leaves in order are outspread
Which ruffling winds shall never shed.
The roses are the magic blue
That in the faery gardens grew,
Not fashioned for themselves alone,
But for the common beauty grown.

They shall not wax, they shall not wane,
They shall not flush to fleet again,
But quaintly, in their quiet place,
Shall charm me with unaltered grace,
And fresh for ever, flower and shoot,
Shall spring from their eternal root.

Margaret Armour

12

Listening to the trees

And the birch says
       it's about dancing and colour

and the rowan says
       it's about berries and birds

and the willow says
       it's about shape and shelter

and the hazel says
       it's about love and lichen

and the aspen says
       it's about growth and the wind

but I say it's about
       listening to the trees

Mandy Haggith

13

River, river

River, river
will you tell me stories?
What did you see on your travels today?

'I saw a fawn standing on a hill top,
and I saw a weasel sliding through a wall.

Then I saw dwarfs with a yellow casket,
and I saw a giant fighting with a bull.'

'I believe about the fawn,
I believe about the weasel,
but not about the dwarfs,
and not about the giant.'

'Well, you asked me for a story,
so I gave you one.
And if you don't believe me
find another stream.'

Iain Crichton Smith

14

Freedom and Love

How delicious is the winning
Of a kiss at love's beginning,
When two mutual hearts are sighing
For the knot there's no untying!

Yet remember, 'midst our wooing,
Love has bliss, but Love has ruing;
Other smiles may make you fickle,
Tears for other charms may trickle.

Love he comes, and Love he tarries,
Just as fate or fancy carries;
Longest stays, when sorest chidden;
Laughs and flies, when press'd and bidden.

Bind the sea to slumber stilly,
Bind its odour to the lily,
Bind the aspen ne'er to quiver,
Then bind Love to last for ever.

Love's a fire that needs renewal
Of fresh beauty for its fuel:
Love's wing moults when caged and captured,
Only free, he soars enraptured.

Can you keep the bee from ranging
Or the ringdove's neck from changing?
No! nor fetter'd Love from dying
In the knot there's no untying.

Thomas Campbell

15

The Trout of the Well

Thou speckled little trout so fair,
The lover of my love, o where?
Is he beyond the ocean's storm,
With heroes holding combat warm?

Thou speckled little trout so fair,
The lover of my mind, o where?
Out on the gloom-hills doth he stride,
Cairn-brownie maiden at his side?

Thou speckled little trout so fair,
The lover of my heart, o where?
The Isle of Youth, is that his bound,
The champions of old around?

Thou speckled little trout so fair,
The lover of my breast, o where?
In Ireland or in Alba steep?
Behind the sun is he asleep?

Thou speckled little trout so fair,
Is with my love MacMary there?
And may I let my sorrow go
In the unfailing River's flow?

Thou speckled little trout so fair,
My lover, o my lover where?

Anon.

16

Lament for Culloden

The lovely lass o' Inverness,
Nae joy nor pleasure can she see;
For e'en and morn she cries, Alas!
And ay the saut tear blin's her e'e:
Drumossie moor – Drumossie day –
A waefu' day it was to me!
For there I lost my father dear,
My father dear, and brethren three.

Their winding-sheet the bluidy clay,
Their graves are growing green to see:
And by them lies the dearest lad
That ever blest a woman's e'e!
Now wae to thee, thou cruel lord,
A bluidy man I trow thou be;
For mony a heart thou hast made sair
That ne'er did wrong to thine or thee.

Robert Burns

17

The Skye Boat Song

Speed bonnie boat like a bird on the wing
Onward the sailors cry
Carry the lad that's born to be king
Over the sea to Skye

Loud the wind howls, loud the waves roar,
Thunderclaps rend the air
Baffled our foes, stand by the shore
Follow they will not dare

Speed bonnie boat like a bird on the wing
Onward the sailors cry
Carry the lad that's born to be king
Over the sea to Skye

Though the waves heave, soft will ye sleep
Ocean's a royal bed
Rocked in the deep, Flora will keep
Watch by your weary head

Speed bonnie boat like a bird on the wing
Onward the sailors cry
Carry the lad that's born to be king
Over the sea to Skye

Many's the lad fought on that day
Well the claymore did wield
When the night came, silently lain
Dead on Culloden field

Speed bonnie boat like a bird on the wing
Onward the sailors cry
Carry the lad that's born to be king
Over the sea to Skye

Burned are our homes, exile and death
Scatter the loyal men
Yet e'er the sword cool in the sheath
Charlie will come again.

Speed bonnie boat like a bird on the wing
Onward the sailors cry
Carry the lad that's born to be king
Over the sea to Skye.

Harold Boulton

18

Celtic Melancholy

It is not in the sorrow of the deep,
For sunset's magic turns to pearls her tears;
Nor in old forests stiff with frost that sleep
Bowed with the legend of her ghostly years;
Nor in the sombre grandeur of the hills,
Whose snows have cold communion with the skies;
Not in the mourning of the moor with rain,
Or solemn mist that spills
Its weariness of silence: or the cries
Of great winds wandering through the glens in pain.

Thou hadst no knowledge of the market-place
And cities white and glad with statuary;
The hiving ports of a far-travelled race,
Idols in gold and jewelled sacristy;
Men hot with story from the ends o' earth,
Plaudits in theatres; an eager fleet
Taking the tide, bound for the goodly wars.
Such stuff of song and mirth
Was never thine amidst the sleet
And noise of black whales spouting to the stars.

Thine is the heritage of wandering men
Whose deeds are fragments passing like the stream;
They build the tower; they forge the shield; and then
Their labours vanish like a fragrant dream.
Wistful and dim with sad magnificence
Ye are the men destined to doom and death.
A purpose ye could never realise;
And stable recompense
Of victory was fleeting as a breath.
Only the face of death is kind and wise.

Ye are the men of perished hopes, of things
Most dear that now are ever lost – home, name,
And country – song of triumph never brings
Like requiem the meaning that's in fame.
Slogan ne'er stirred the heart to dare and die
As coronach loud wailing in the glen.
Ah! aye for you the best's beneath the sod;
Over the sea to Skye;
All's over; falls the night on broken men,
Culloden's sword with blood writes Ichabod.

John MacDougall Hay

19

To a Mountain Daisy

On turning one down with the plough in April 1786

Wee, modest, crimson-tippèd flow'r,
Thou's met me in an evil hour;
For I maun crush amang the stoure
   Thy slender stem:
To spare thee now is past my pow'r,
   Thou bonnie gem.

Alas! it's no thy neebor sweet,
The bonnie lark, companion meet,
Bending thee 'mang the dewy weet,
   Wi' spreckl'd breast,
When upward-springing, blythe to greet
   The purpling east.

Cauld blew the bitter-biting north
Upon thy early, humble birth;
Yet cheerfully thou glinted forth
   Amid the storm,
Scarce rear'd above the parent earth
   Thy tender form.

The flaunting flow'rs our gardens yield,
High sheltering woods and wa's maun shield;
But thou, beneath the random bield
    O cold or stane,
Adorns the histie stibble-field,
    Unseen, alane.

There, in thy scanty mantle clad,
Thy snawy bosom sun-ward spread,
Thou lifts thy unassuming head
    In humble guise;
But now the share uptears thy bed,
    And low thou lies!

Such is the fate of artless maid,
Sweet flowret of the rural shade!
By love's simplicity betray'd,
    And guileless trust,
Till she, like thee, all soil'd, is laid
    Low i' the dust.

Such is the fate of simple bard,
On life's rough ocean luckless starr'd!
Unskilful he to note the card
    Of prudent lore,
Till billows rage, and gales blow hard,
    And whelm him o'er!

Such fate to suffering worth is giv'n,
Who long with wants and woes has striv'n,
By human pride or cunning driv'n
    To mis'ry's brink,
Till, wrench'd of ev'ry stay but Heav'n,
    He, ruin'd, sink!

Ev'n thou who mourn'st the Daisy's fate,
That fate is thine – no distant date;
Stern Ruin's ploughshare drives, elate,
    Full on thy bloom,
Till, crush'd beneath the furrow's weight,
    Shall be thy doom!

Robert Burns

20

Sassenachs

Me and my best pal (well, she was
till a minute ago) are off to London.
First trip on an intercity alone.
When we got on we were the same
kind of excited – jigging on our seats,
staring at everyone. But then,
I remembered I had to be sophisticated.
So when Jenny started shouting,
'Look at that, the land's flat already,'
when we were just outside Glasgow
(Motherwell actually) I'd feel myself flush.
Or even worse, 'Sassenach country!
Wey Hey Hey.' The tartan tammy
sitting proudly on top of her pony;
the tartan scarf swinging like a tail.
The nose pressed to the window.
'England's not so beautiful, is it?'
And we haven't even crossed the border!
And the train's jazzy beat joins her:
Sassenachs Sassenachs here we come.
Sassenachs Sassenachs Rum Tum Tum
Sassenachs Sassenachs How do you do.
Sassenachs Sassenachs WE'LL GET YOU.

Then she loses momentum, so out come
the egg mayonnaise sandwiches and
the big bottle of Bru. 'My ma's done us proud,'
says Jenny, digging in, munching loud.
The whole train is an egg and I'm inside it.
I try to remain calm; Jenny starts it again,
Sassenachs Sassenachs Rum Tum Tum.

Finally we get there: London, Euston;
and the first person on the platform
gets asked – 'Are you a genuine Sassenach?'
I want to die, but instead I say, *'Jenny!'*
He replies in that English way –
'I beg your pardon,' and Jenny screams
'Did you hear that Voice?'
And we both die laughing, clutching
our stomachs at Euston.

Jackie Kay

21

from Childe Harold's Pilgrimage

There is a pleasure in the pathless woods,
There is a rapture on the lonely shore,
There is society, where none intrudes,
By the deep Sea, and music in its roar:
I love not Man the less, but Nature more,
From these our interviews, in which I steal
From all I may be, or have been before,
To mingle with the Universe, and feel
What I can ne'er express, yet cannot all conceal.

George Gordon, Lord Byron

22

Mary Morison

O Mary, at thy window be,
It is the wish'd, the trysted hour!
Those smiles and glances let me see
That make the miser's treasure poor:
How blithely wad I bide the stoure,
A weary slave frae sun to sun;
Could I the rich reward secure,
The lovely Mary Morison.

Yestreen, when to the trembling string,
The dance gaed through the lighted ha',
To thee my fancy took its wing –
I sat, but neither heard nor saw:
Though this was fair, and that was braw,
And yon the toast of a' the town,
I sigh'd, and said, amang them a',
'Ye are na Mary Morison.'

O Mary, canst thou wreck his peace
Wha for thy sake wad gladly die?
Or canst thou break that heart of his
Wha's only faut is loving thee?
If love for love thou wilt na gie,
At least be pity on me shown;
A thought ungentle canna be
The thought o' Mary Morison.

Robert Burns

23

Will Ye No Come Back Again?

Will ye no come back again?
Will ye no come back again?
Better lo'ed ye canna be,
Will ye no come back again?

Bonnie Charlie's now awa,
    Safely owre the friendly main;
Mony a heart will break in twa,
    Should he ne'er come back again.

Ye trusted in your Hieland men,
    They trusted you, dear Charlie;
They kent you hiding in the glen,
    Your cleadin' was but barely.

English bribes were a' in vain;
    An' e'en tho' puirer we may be,
Siller canna buy the heart
    That beats aye for thine and thee.

We watched thee in the gloaming hour,
    We watched thee in the morning grey;
Tho' thirty thousand pounds they'd gie,
    Oh there is nane that wad betray.

Sweet's the laverock's note and lang,
   Lilting wildly up the glen;
But aye to me he sings ae sang, –
   Will ye no come back again?

Will ye no come back again?
Will ye no come back again?
Better lo'ed ye canna be,
Will ye no come back again?

Carolina Oliphant, Lady Nairne

24

Spring Song

About the flowerless land adventurous bees
    Pickeering hum; the rooks debate, divide,
    With many a hoarse aside,
In solemn conclave on the budding trees;
Larks in the skies and plough-boys o'er the leas
Carol as if the winter never had been;
    The very owl comes out to greet the sun;
    Rivers high hearted run;
And hedges mantle with a flush of green.

The curlew calls me where the salt winds blow;
    His troubled note dwells mournfully and dies;
    Then the long echo cries
Deep in my heart. Ah, surely I must go!
For there the tides, moon-haunted, ebb and flow;
And there the seaboard murmurs resonant;
    The waves their interwoven fugue repeat
    And brooding surges beat
A slow, melodious, continual chant.

John Davidson

Shepherdess

All day my sheep have mingled with yours. They strayed
Into your valley seeking a change of ground.
Held and bemused with what they and I had found,
Pastures and wonders, heedlessly I delayed.
Now it is late. The tracks leading home are steep,
The stars and landmarks in your country are strange.
How can I take my sheep back over the range?
Shepherdess, show me now where I may sleep.

Norman Cameron

26

Wee Davie Daylicht

Wee Davie Daylicht keeks owre the sea,
Early in the mornin', wi' a clear e'e;
Waukens a' the birdies that are sleepin' soun'.
Wee Davie Daylicht is nae lazy loon.

Wee Davie Daylicht glow'rs owre the hill,
Glints through the greenwood, dances on the rill;
Smiles on the wee cot, shines on the ha';
Wee Davie Daylicht cheers the hearts o' a'.

Come bonnie bairnie, come awa' to me;
Cuddle in my bosie, sleep upon my knee.
Wee Davie Daylicht noo has closed his e'e.
In amang the rosy clouds, far ayont the sea.

Robert Tenant

Summit of Corrie Etchachan

But in the climbing ecstasy of thought,
Ere consummation, ere the final peak,
Come hours like this. Behind, the long defile,
The steep rock-path, alongside which, from under
Snow-caves, sharp-corniced, tumble the ice-cold waters.
And now, here, at the corrie's summit, no peak,
No vision of the blue world, far, unattainable,
But this grey plateau, rock-strewn, vast, silent,
The dark loch, the toiling crags, the snow;
A mountain shut within itself, yet a world,
Immensity. So may the mind achieve,
Toiling, no vision of the infinite,
But a vast, dark and inscrutable sense
Of its own terror, its own glory and power.

Nan Shepherd

28

The Flowers of Scotland

What are the flowers of Scotland,
　　All others that excel –
The lovely flowers of Scotland,
　　All others that excel?
The thistle's purple bonnet,
　　And bonny heather-bell,
O, they're the flowers of Scotland,
　　All others that excel!

Though England eyes her roses
　　With pride she'll ne'er forgo,
The rose has oft been trodden
　　By foot of haughty foe;
But the thistle in her bonnet blue
　　Still nods outow'r the fell,
And dares the proudest foeman
　　To tread the heather-bell.

For the wee bit leaf o' Ireland,
　　Alack and well a-day!
For ilka hand is free to pu'
　　An' steal the gem away.
But the thistle in her bonnet blue
　　Still bobs aboon them a';
At her the bravest darena blink,
　　Or gi'e his mou' a thraw.

Up wi' the flowers o' Scotland,
    The emblem o' the free,
Their guardians for a thousand years,
    Their guardians still we'll be.
A foe had better brave the deil
    Within his reeky cell,
Than our thistle's purple-bonnet,
    Or bonny heather-bell.

James Hogg

A Boy's Song

Where the pools are bright and deep,
Where the grey trout lies asleep,
Up the river and o'er the lea,
That's the way for Billy and me.

Where the blackbird sings the latest,
Where the hawthorn blooms the sweetest,
Where the nestlings plentiest be,
That's the way for Billy and me.

Where the mowers mow the cleanest,
Where the hay lies thick and greenest,
There to trace the homeward bee,
That's the way for Billy and me.

Where the poplar grows the smallest,
Where the old pine waves the tallest,
'Pies and rooks know who are we,
That's the way for Billy and me.

Where the hazel bank is steepest,
Where the shadow falls the deepest,
Where the clustering nuts fall free,
That's the way for Billy and me.

Why the boys should drive away
Little sweet maidens from the play,
Or love to tear and fight so well,
That's the thing I never could tell.

But this I know, I love to play
Through the meadow, among the hay;
Up the water and o'er the lea,
That's the way for Billy and me.

James Hogg

30

We used to think the universe was made . . .

We used to think the universe was made
of tiny invisible pin-points of energy, jostling
and tumbling and buzzing together, and so,
by whatever particular arrangement they took,
and the way in which they bounced off one another,
all sorts of physical matter could be produced.
Later we found the universe, in actual fact, is made
of tiny invisible threads of incredible length, and,

in the same way a violin string changes pitch
when touched at points along its measured span,
so all these interweaving loops and knots,
this tangle of quantum spaghetti,
as it flexes and line crosses line,
so it resonates throughout the whole bundle
a complex vibratory code that defines
any outward appearance and characteristic.

After which we discovered the likely reality
was of tiny invisible sheets, many layers
of infinitesimal thinness, each film
undulating at tremendous speeds;
multiple parallel oceans, their rippling surfaces
folding and flattening, wave-crests on wave-crests,
nudged at and nosed at, their lingering kisses
collected, expressed as specific material forms.

We were young, we were anxious to clutch at
whatever proof fitted. Still, humility liberates;
when it comes to matters of truth we're not picky.
Ironing our numbers presented the ideal
of tiny invisible shapeshifting blocks that squirm
and bulge, interlock and uncouple, that rub,
knock, wobble, split, and so make up
the whole gamut of substances we take for granted.

All this was long ago. Our models had risen
to eleven-dimensional-space when
our application for further funding was rejected
and we were asked to vacate the premises.
We took it well, were optimistic for the future,
though that was hardly the crux of the issue:
just try transporting eleven-dimensional furniture
in an incontrovertibly three-dimensional van.

J. O. Morgan

May

I

I Will Make You Brooches

I will make you brooches and toys for your delight
Of bird-song at morning and star-shine at night.
I will make a palace fit for you and me
Of green days in forests and blue days at sea.

I will make my kitchen, and you shall keep your room,
Where white flows the river and bright blows the broom,
And you shall wash your linen and keep your body white
In rainfall at morning and dewfall at night.

And this shall be for music when no one else is near,
The fine song for singing, the rare song to hear!
That only I remember, that only you admire,
Of the broad road that stretches and the roadside fire.

Robert Louis Stevenson

2

coire fhionn lochan

lapping of the little waves
breaking of the little waves
spreading of the little waves
idling of the little waves

rippling of the little waves
settling of the little waves
meeting of the little waves
swelling of the little waves

trembling of the little waves
dancing of the little waves
pausing of the little waves
slanting of the little waves

tossing of the little waves
scribbling of the little waves
lilting of the little waves
sparkling of the little waves

leaping of the little waves
drifting of the little waves
running of the little waves
splashing of the little waves

Thomas A. Clark

3

For a Wedding

Camilla and Kieran 9/8/94

Cousin, I think the shape of a marriage
is like the shelves my parents have carried
through Scotland to London, three houses;

is not distinguished, fine, French-polished,
but plywood and tatty, made
in the first place for children to batter,

still carrying markings in green felt tip,
but always, where there are books
and a landing, managing to fit;

that marriage has lumps like
their button-backed sofa, constantly,
shortly, about to be stuffed;

and that love grows fat
as their squinting cat, swelling
round as a loaf from her basket.

I wish you years that shape, that form,
and a pond in a Sunday, urban garden;
where you'll see your joined reflection tremble,

stand and watch the waterboatmen
skate with ease across the surface tension.

Kate Clanchy

4

The cock an the hen

The cock an the hen,
The deer in the den,
Sail drink in the clearest fountain.

The venison rare
Sall be ma love's fare,
An A'll follow him ower the mountain.

Anon.

5

Aunt Julia

Aunt Julia spoke Gaelic
very loud and very fast.
I could not answer her –
I could not understand her.

She wore men's boots
when she wore any.
– I can see her strong foot,
stained with peat,
paddling with the treadle of the spinningwheel
while her right hand drew yarn
marvellously out of the air.

Hers was the only house
where I've lain at night
in the absolute darkness
of a box bed, listening to
crickets being friendly.

She was buckets
and water flouncing into them.
She was winds pouring wetly
round house-ends.
She was brown eggs, black skirts
and a keeper of threepennybits
in a teapot.

Aunt Julia spoke Gaelic
very loud and very fast.
By the time I had learned
a little, she lay
silenced in the absolute black
of a sandy grave
at Luskentyre.
But I hear her still, welcoming me
with a seagull's voice
across a hundred yards
of peatscapes and lazybeds
and getting angry, getting angry
with so many questions
unanswered.

Norman MacCaig

6

The Hill

So it may be a hill was there,
    Blue, tremulous, afar.
I looked and thought the gleam was air,
    And thought the morning star

Might tremble thus and thus resolve
    Its fire in common light,
Content, while world and sun revolve,
    To vanish from the sight.

So hard it was that morn to tell
    If earth or heaven saw,
I knew not how on earth to dwell
    Nor how from heaven withdraw.

For vanishing within my thought,
    And stealing back to view,
Earth mingled so with heaven, they wrought
    One universe from two.

Nan Shepherd

Particle Poems: 3

Three particles lived in mystical union.
They made knife, fork, and spoon,
and earth, sea, and sky.
They made animal, vegetable, and mineral,
and faith, hope, and charity.
They made stop, caution, go,
and hickory, dickory, dock.
They made yolk, white, and shell,
and hook, line, and sinker.
They made pounds, shillings, and pence,
and Goneril, Regan, and Cordelia.
They made Shadrach, Meshach, and Abednego,
and game, set, and match.

A wandering particle captured one of them,
and the two that were left made day and night,
and left and right, and right and wrong,
and black and white, and off and on,
but things were never quite the same,
and two will always yearn for three.
They're after you, or me.

Edwin Morgan

8

Loch Lomond

By yon bonnie banks and by yon bonnie braes
Where the sun shines bright on Loch Lomond
Where me and my true love were ever wont tae gae
On the bonnie, bonnie banks o' Loch Lomond.

Oh you tak' the high road and I'll tak the low road
An' I'll be in Scotland afore ye,
But me and my true love will never meet again
On the bonnie, bonnie banks o' Loch Lomond.

'Twas there that we parted in yon shady glen
On the steep, steep side of Ben Lomond,
Where in purple hue, the hieland hills we view,
And the moon comin' out in the gloamin'.

Oh you tak' the high road and I'll tak the low road
And I'll be in Scotland afore ye,
But me and my true love will never meet again
On the bonnie, bonnie banks o' Loch Lomond.

The wee birdies sing, and the wild flowers spring,
While in sunshine the waters are sleeping
But the broken heart it kens nae second spring again,
Tho' the waefu' may cease free their greetin'.

Oh you tak' the high road and I'll tak the low road
An' I'll be in Scotland afore ye,
But me and my true love will never meet again
On the bonnie, bonnie banks o' Loch Lomond.

Alicia Ann, Lady John Scott

9

The Northern Islands

In favoured summers
These islands have the sun all to themselves
And light a toy to play with, weeks on end.
The empty sky and waters are a shell
Endlessly turning, turning the wheel of light,
While the tranced waves run wavering up the sand.
The beasts sleep when they can, midnight or midday,
Slumbering on into the unending brightness.
The green, green fields give too much, are too rank
With beautiful beasts for breeding or for slaughter.
The horses, glorious useless race, are leaving.
Have the old ways left with them, and the faith,
Lost in this dream too comfortable and goodly
To make room for a blessing? Where can it fall?
The old ways change in the turning, turning light,
Taking and giving life to life from life.

Edwin Muir

10

Songs of my Native Land

Songs of my native land,
To me how dear!
Songs of my infancy,
Sweet to mine ear!
Entwined with my youthful days,
Wi' the bonny banks and braes,
Where the winding burnie strays
Murmuring near.

Strains of thy native land,
That thrill the soul,
Pouring the magic of
Your soft control!
Often has your minstrelsy
Soothed the pangs of misery,
Winging rapid thoughts away
To realms on high.

Weary pilgrims there have rest,
Their wand'rings o'er;
There the slave, no more oppress'd,
Hails Freedom's shore.
Sin shall then no more deface,
Sickness, pain, and sorrow cease,
Ending in eternal peace,
And songs of joy!

There, when the seraphs sing,
In cloudless day;
There, where the higher praise
The ransom'd pay.
Soft strains of the happy land,
Chanted by the heavenly band,
Who can fully understand
How sweet ye be!

Carolina Oliphant, Lady Nairne

11

Where Go the Boats?

Dark brown is the river,
  Golden is the sand.
It flows along for ever,
  With trees on either hand.

Green leaves a-floating,
  Castles of the foam,
Boats of mine a-boating –
  Where will all come home?

On goes the river
  And out past the mill,
Away down the valley,
  Away down the hill.

Away down the river,
  A hundred miles or more,
Other little children
  Shall bring my boats ashore.

Robert Louis Stevenson

12

Scotland

Semiconductor country, land crammed with intimate
    expanses,
Your cities are superlattices, heterojunctive
Graphed from the air, your cropmarked farmlands
Are epitaxies of tweed.

All night motorways carry your signal, swept
To East Kilbride or Dunfermline. A brightness off low
    headlands
Beams-in the dawn to Fife's interstices,
Optoelectronics of hay.

Micro-nation. So small you cannot be forgotten,
Bible inscribed on a ricegrain, hi-tech's key
Locked into the earth, your televised Glasgows
Are broadcast in Rio. Among circuitboard crowsteps

To be miniaturised is not small-minded.
To love you needs more detail than the Book of Kells –
Your harbours, your photography, your democratic intellect
Still boundless, chip of a nation.

Robert Crawford

13

To the Evening Star

Star that bringest home the bee,
And sett'st the weary labourer free!
If any star shed peace, 'tis Thou
   That send'st it from above,
Appearing when Heaven's breath and brow
   Are sweet as hers we love.

Come to the luxuriant skies,
Whilst the landscape's odours rise,
Whilst far-off lowing herds are heard
   And songs when toil is done,
From cottages whose smoke unstirr'd
   Curls yellow in the sun.

Star of love's soft interviews,
Parted lovers on thee muse;
Their remembrancer in Heaven
   Of thrilling vows thou art,
Too delicious to be riven
   By absence from the heart.

                        Thomas Campbell

14

Sing me a Song of a Lad that is Gone

Mull was astern, Rum on the port,
Eigg on the starboard bow;
Glory of youth glowed in his soul:
Where is that glory now?

Chorus
    Sing me a song of a lad that is gone,
    Say, could that lad be I?
    Merry of soul he sailed on a day
    Over the sea to Skye.

Give me again all that was there,
Give me the sun that shone!
Give me the eyes, give me the soul,
Give me that lad that's gone!

Chorus

Billow and breeze, islands and seas,
Mountains of rain and sun,
All that was good, all that was fair,
All that was me is gone.

Chorus

        Robert Louis Stevenson

15

In My Country

walking by the waters
down where an honest river
shakes hands with the sea,
a woman passed round me
in a slow watchful circle,
as if I were a superstition;

or the worst dregs of her imagination,
so when she finally spoke
her words spliced into bars
of an old wheel. A segment of air.
Where do you come from?
'Here,' I said, 'Here. These parts.'

Jackie Kay

16

Autistic

You feel you cannot reach
                        me.
You feel that I'm
                        adrift,
A small boat lost on your
Enormous sea.
But I *can* hear you,
                        just,
As sailors hear mermaids sing
On the edge of the horizon.
I can see you
        far away,
A coppery, spinning coin
Which slips between the inky ocean
And the darkening sky.
Wait.
I am busy
Studying this shell,
Remembering its shape
With my fingertips.
I am happy
Under its spell.

Lindsay MacRae

17

Mary of Argyll

I have heard the mavis singing
His love song to the morn,
I have seen the dewdrop clinging
To the rose but newly born.
But a sweeter song has cheer'd me
At the evening's gentle close,
And I've seen an eye still brighter
Than the dewdrop on the rose.
'Twas thy voice, my gentle Mary,
And thy artless winning smile,
That made this world an Eden,
Bonny Mary of Argyll.

Tho' thy voice may lose its sweetness
And thine eye its brightness too,
Tho' thy step may lack its fleetness
And thy hair its sunny hue,
Still to me wilt thou be dearer
Than all the world shall own,
I have loved thee for thy beauty
But not for that alone.
I have watched thy heart, dear Mary,
And its goodness was the wile
That has made thee mine forever,
Bonny Mary of Argyll.

Charles Jefferys

18

Bright is the Ring of Words

Bright is the ring of words
When the right man rings them,
Fair the fall of songs
When the singer sings them.
Still they are carolled and said –
On wings they are carried –
After the singer is dead
And the maker buried.

Low as the singer lies
In the field of heather,
Songs of his fashion bring
The swains together.
And when the west is red
With the sunset embers,
The lover lingers and sings
And the maid remembers.

Robert Louis Stevenson

19

Highland Landscape

Here, there is beauty every sense can share
Against the moving backcloth of the sky;
The murmur of the stream, the scented air,
The various enchantments for the eye.
About my feet the moor is yellow-starred
With tormentil, the friendliest of flowers;
Above, the mighty peak that stands on guard
Forms and dissolves between the passing showers.
Wherever near or far the eye may dwell,
All things contribute to a sense of fitness
So integral, it would be hard to tell
Which of them bears the more impressive witness –
The splendid sweep of the enclosing hill,
The neat perfection of the tormentil.

Douglas J. Fraser

20

Cairngorm Seedlings

Once upon an autumn day, they were
three tiny seedlings, carried down the track
from Whitehaugh, Glen Clova Forest way.
Thinking ahead about their welfare
I shouldered a wee poly bag of gritty soil.

Just as well. It was to be the last hill walk,
followed by a final homeward drive.
The year? 2008, my *annus horribilis*,
eyesight, hindsight, balance sore impeded.
But those three seedlings were well seeded . . .

A simple pleasure now is noting mere survival
ten winters since that long-remembered day.
Those 'bonsai' plants of pine, larch, yew, all
flourish still: albeit still too small to emit much smell
of damp, snug, montane grit in mossy pots of clay.

Gordon Jarvie

21

Conundrum

You'd think there would be a neat equation for how
when travelling by train the view from the window
and in the mirror opposite make clear we are hurtling
away from the past, and into our future, at precisely

the same speed. Simple you say, stating the obvious.
But it doesn't explain how images, as they recede,
may enlarge in the memory; tunnels ahead shorten
or lengthen in accordance with changes of mood.

Even more how an intrusive cell or invisible speck
between sets of nerves can have an impact more
catastrophic than a rock fissure in a mountain ravine;
the tremor of an eyelid, cataclysmic as any fault-line.

Stewart Conn

22

The Bonny Muir Hen

The bonny muir hen
Has feathers enoo,
The bonny muir hen
Has feathers enoo.

There's some o' them black,
An there's some o' them blue,
The bonny muir hen
Has feathers enoo.

Anon.

23

Patagonia

I said perhaps Patagonia, and pictured
a peninsula, wide enough
for a couple of ladderback chairs
to wobble on at high tide. I thought
of us in breathless cold, facing
a horizon round as a coin, looped
in a cat's cradle strung by gulls
from sea to sun. I planned to wait
till the waves had bored themselves
to sleep, till the last clinging barnacles,
growing worried in the hush, had
paddled off in tiny coracles, till
those restless birds, your actor's hands,
had dropped slack into your lap,
until you'd turned, at last, to me.
When I spoke of Patagonia, I meant
skies all empty aching blue. I meant
years. I meant all of them with you.

Kate Clanchy

24

John Anderson my Jo

John Anderson my jo, John,
When we were first acquent;
Your locks were like the raven,
Your bonny brow was brent;
But now your brow is beld, John,
Your locks are like the snow;
But blessings on your frosty pow,
John Anderson my jo.

John Anderson my jo, John,
We clamb the hill thegither;
And mony a canty day, John,
We've had wi' ane anither:
Now we maun totter doun, John,
And hand in hand we'll go,
And sleep thegither at the foot,
John Anderson my jo.

Robert Burns

25

The Whales

If I could stand the pressures,
if I could make myself strong,

I'd dive far under the ocean,
away from these merfolk

– especially the mermen, moaning
and wringing out their beards.

I'd discover a cave
green and ventricular

and there, with tremendous patience,
I'd teach myself to listen:

what the whale-fish hear
answering through the vastnesses

I'd hear too. But oh my love,
tell me you'd swim by,

tell me you'd look out for me,
down there it's impossible to breathe –

Kathleen Jamie

26

Weather Rhyme from Angus

Geese tae the sea, guid weather tae be;
Geese tae the hull, guid weather tae spill.

Anon.

27

Orkney: The Whale Islands

Sharp spindrift struck
At prow's turning.
Then the helmsman,
'Either whales to starboard
Or this storm
Is thrusting us at Thule,
Neighbour to bergs, beneath
The boreal star.'
Sunset. We furled ship
In a wide sea-loch.
Star-harrows
Went over our thin sleep.
Dawn. A rainbow crumbled
Over Orc, 'whale islands'.
Then the skipper, 'The whales
Will yield this folk
Corn and fleeces and honey.'
And the poet,
'Harp of whalebone, shake
Golden words from my mouth.'

George Mackay Brown

28

The time traivellers' convention

Bring a pairtner tae the Ceilidh
Dress informal, the invite stated
At the time traivellers' convention.

Mary Queen o Scots arrived hersel
Signed up fur speed-datin.
Said she wis a romantic,
Cud lose her heid ower the richt chiel.

The sheik in the tartan troosers
Turned oot tae be Rabbie Burns
Wi a bevy o beauties he'd gaithered
On his traivels.

John Knox tuik charge o the raffle
The kirk being eesed tae collectin
Naebody socht him fur a lady's choice.

Lord Byron niver missed a single dance
In the Gay Gordons. He wis last tae leave.

The Loch Ness Monster, playin watter music
Last seen wis reelin roon bi Ailsa Crag
Wi thirteen kelpies and a Shetlan silkie.

Feedback suggests they'll aa be back neist year.

Sheena Blackhall

29

This Poem . . .

This poem is dangerous: it should not be left
Within the reach of children, or even of adults
Who might swallow it whole, with possibly
Undesirable side-effects. If you come across
An unattended, unidentified poem
In a public place, do not attempt to tackle it
Yourself. Send it (preferably, in a sealed container)
To the nearest centre of learning, where it will be rendered
Harmless, by experts. Even the simplest poem
May destroy your immunity to human emotions.
All poems must carry a Government warning. Words
Can seriously affect your heart.

Elma Mitchell

Fax

Tha 'm fax anns an oisean
Na thrèan-ri-trèan anns a' chluain

No na mhuc a' gnòsail
Ann an guth ìseal

Is tha 'm printer taobh ris na leum na eas
Agus duilleagan bàn' a' sruthadh às

Is tha seallaidhean gan sgrìobadh
A chaidh a dhraghadh

A grinneal a' Chuain Siair
Air sgàilean m'annalair

'S iad uile cur an cruth fhèin gu seòlta
Air saoghal an latha.

Rody Gorman

Fax

The fax in the corner
is a corncrake in the meadow

or a pig grunting
in a low voice

and the printer beside it is a waterfall
with white pages gushing out of it

and scenes are being depicted
that were trawled

from the bed of the Atlantic
on the screen of my computer

and they all put their own form neatly
on today's world.

Rody Gorman

31

Basking Shark

To stub an oar on a rock where none should be,
To have it rise with a slounge out of the sea
Is a thing that happened once (too often) to me.

But not too often – though enough. I count as gain
That once I met, on a sea tin-tacked with rain,
That roomsized monster with a matchbox brain.

He displaced more than water. He shoggled me
Centuries back – this decadent townee
Shook on a wrong branch of his family tree.

Swish up the dirt and, when it settles, a spring
Is all the clearer. I saw me, in one fling,
Emerging from the slime of everything.

So who's the monster? The thought made me grow pale
For twenty seconds while, sail after sail,
The tall fin slid away and then the tail.

Norman MacCaig

June

I

How many sailors to sail a ship?

One with a broken heart
to weep sad buckets.

One with an arrowed heart
tattooed on a bicep.

Two with four blue eyes
to mirror the sea.

Two with four blue eyes
to mirror the sky.

One with a salty tongue
to swear at a pirate.

One with a baby's caul
to keep from a-drowning.

Two with four green eyes
to mirror the sea.

Two with four grey eyes
to mirror the sky.

One with a wooden leg
to dance on a gangplank.

One with a flask of rum
to gargle at midnight.

Two with four grey eyes
to mirror the sea.

Two with four black eyes
to mirror the sky.

Luff! Leech! Clew! Tack!
Off to sea! Won't be back!

Luff! Clew! Tack! Leech!
Off to sea! No more beach!

One with an albatross
to put in a poem.

Two with four blue eyes
to mirror the sea.

One with a secret map
to stitch in a lining.

Two with four grey eyes
to mirror the sea.

One with a violin
to scrape at a dolphin.

Two with four green eyes
to mirror the sea.

Luff! Leech! Tack! Clew!
Off to sea! Yo ho! Adieu!

One with a telescope
to clock the horizon.

Two with four blue eyes
to mirror the sky.

One with a yard of rope
to lasso a tempest.

Two with four grey eyes
to mirror the sky.

One with a heavy heart
to sink for an anchor.

Two with four black eyes
to mirror the sky.

Leech! Clew! Tack! Luff!
Off to sea! We've had enough!

Carol Ann Duffy

2

She Walks in Beauty

She walks in beauty, like the night
   Of cloudless climes and starry skies;
And all that's best of dark and bright
   Meet in her aspect and her eyes;
Thus mellowed to that tender light
   Which heaven to gaudy day denies.

One shade the more, one ray the less,
   Had half impaired the nameless grace
Which waves in every raven tress,
   Or softly lightens o'er her face;
Where thoughts serenely sweet express
   How pure, how dear their dwelling-place.

And on that cheek, and o'er that brow,
   So soft, so calm, yet eloquent,
That smiles that win, the tints that glow,
   But tell of the days in goodness spent,
A mind at peace with all below,
   A heart whose love is innocent!

George Gordon, Lord Byron

3

Litany of Time Past

What's today?
  Hoops today.
What's yesterday?
  Tops yesterday.
What's tomorrow?
  Diabolo.

Moons and planets come out to play,
The Bear bowled, the Sun spun.
See the Devil-on-sticks run
Today, tomorrow, and yesterday.

What's Hope?
  Skipping rope.
What's Clarity?
  Salty peppery.
What's Faith?
  Edinburgh, Leith,
  Portobello, Musselburgh,
  and Dalkeith.

Out you are.
  In you are.
Mustard.
  Vinegar.

Muriel Spark

4

The Braes of Yarrow

Thy braes were bonny, Yarrow stream,
When first on them I met my lover;
Thy braes how dreary, Yarrow stream,
When now thy waves his body cover!
For ever now, O Yarrow stream!
Thou art to me a stream of sorrow;
For never on thy banks shall I
Behold my Love, the flower of Yarrow.

He promised me a milk-white steed
To bear me to his father's bowers;
He promised me a little page
To squire me to his father's towers;
He promised me a wedding-ring, –
The wedding-day was fix'd to-morrow; –
Now he is wedded to his grave,
Alas, his watery grave, in Yarrow!

Sweet were his words when last we met;
My passion I as freely told him;
Clasp'd in his arms, I little thought
That I should never more behold him!
Scarce was he gone, I saw his ghost;
It vanish'd with a shriek of sorrow;
Thrice did the water-wraith ascend,
And gave a doleful groan thro' Yarrow.

His mother from the window look'd
With all the longing of a mother;
His little sister weeping walk'd
The green-wood path to meet her brother;
They sought him east, they sought him west,
They sought him all the forest thorough;
They only saw the cloud of night,
They only heard the roar of Yarrow.

No longer from thy window look –
Thou hast no son, thou tender mother!
No longer walk, thou lovely maid;
Alas, thou hast no more a brother!
No longer seek him east or west
And search no more the forest thorough;
For, wandering in the night so dark,
He fell a lifeless corpse in Yarrow.

The tear shall never leave my cheek,
No other youth shall be my marrow –
I'll seek thy body in the stream,
And then with thee I'll sleep in Yarrow.
– The tear did never leave her cheek,
No other youth became her marrow;
She found his body in the stream,
And now with him she sleeps in Yarrow.

John Logan

5

Rain

The rain is raining all around,
  It falls on field and tree,
It rains on the umbrellas here,
  And on the ships at sea.

Robert Louis Stevenson

6

Oak Branch and Tree Warbler

After Shotei Hiroaki

Tiny bird perilous on pencil thin branch,
sure as she can be in this floating world.
Hard acorns drop into the still loch.
Even atoms are mostly absence,
electrons circling like birds
never coming in to roost.

Samuel Tongue

Walking in the Botanic Gardens, Glasgow

For my sisters, Carole and Pam

I think about the folk that went before,
led full lives near this place but are no more.
I picture two small girls astride a brand-new, shiny trike;
one's sixty now and getting wobbly on her bike . . .
The sun still shines, the clouds still race and pass,
the flowers still bloom and lovers lie upon the grass.
The traffic on Great Western Road is constant now,
and I am old and sport a wrinkled brow.

The same trees stretch their arms towards the sky;
they've kept their figures better far than I.
I watch a toddler run beside his dad;
why do they make me feel alive and glad?
Maybe because in them I'm forced to see
life's onward cycle, for – not once but twice thus far –
that toddler and his dad were me.

Gordon Jarvie

8

The Unicorn Seat

for Elsie and Lucy who once had such a magical place

The night is warm and we walk down
the winding track, under a green-lit
tunnel of trees. I have one little hand

in each of mine and you both stare up
at the arching evening. The fantastical
birds swoop down, flashing their magical

plumage, outstretching wings of scarlet,
azure, gold and green. They are our guardians.
They will watch over two girls and a woman

making their way to the small, battered seat
with their unicorn, led by its silken halter
which, tonight, is mauve,

the colour of storms when the worst
has passed and the light is reasserting itself.
We stop by the bench and I wipe rainwater

from the slats. You untie our gentle companion.
Don't worry, you tell me. *She never strays very far
and she always comes back to us.*

Tracey Herd

9

Memorial of St Columba

Mouth of the dumb,
light of the blind,
foot of the lame,
to the fallen stretch out your hand.
Strengthen the senseless,
restore the mad.
O Columba, hope of Scots,
by your merits' mediation
make us companions
of the blessed angels.
    Alleluia.

Anon.,
translated by Gilbert Márkus

10

For W. S. Graham

Sydney, I took a pint of Tinner's Ale
as you took yours: down at the pub at sunset light
when the Zennor sea grows fiercely blue

round this windblown spit of knotted land
where you fled from the knuckled whack of the Clyde,
ran into the lap of the lazy Atlantic.

Was it here that language had you in its clasp,
tossed you like a slip of driftwood on an ocean,
caught you in its net like silvered mackerel?

Did it nip at your tongue on winter days
as you strode the icy edges of the cliffs
and cranked your frozen bones with whisky?

Did it enter your skin when spring came in
with the flecks of blossom, the cuckoo-spit,
the honeyed smell of bluebells in the woods?

Did it spin in your head in sun-plumped summer
when Zennor meadows grow drowsy with bees
and hedgeflowers spill tipsily into the lanes?

Did it hurtle about you in blackberry autumn
when bold winds blow in from the end of the land,
making you cower from the gale and growl of it

down by Madron where the rain in the trees
lulls you to sleep in the wide-eyed dawn
when sea is milky-green and dreams are fleet

and fat with words and you wake with a salt taste
on your tongue? Was this how it had you, Sydney,
all those years? And was the ale always this good,

this golden?

Elizabeth Burns

11

Sing, sing!

Sing, sing!
Whit sall A sing?
The cat ran awa
Wi ma apron string.

Anon.

12

Application

O let me be your bidie-in
And keep you close within
As dearest kith and kin
I promise I'd be tidy in
Whatever bed or bunk you're in
I'd never ever drink your gin
I'd be your multi-vitamin
I'd wear my sexy tiger-skin
And play my love-sick mandolin
It cannot be a mortal sin
To be in such a dizzy spin
I'd like to get inside your skin
I'd even be your concubine
I hope you know I'm genuine
O let me be your bidie-in.

Diana Hendry

13

Appointment

Of course, you may be my bidie-in,
You didn't need to apply within.
A braw new world's about to begin,
We'll gang thegether through thick and thin,
We'll walk unscathed through burr and whin.
If you're to be my porcupin
I'll just have to bear it and grin.
I'll be your sheik, your djinn,
I'll be yang to your yin.
You'll be my kitten, my mitten, my terrapin.
All night long we'll make love's sweet din
And never mind the wheelie-bin.
In our romantic cin-
ema there'll be no FIN.
And so I say again – you're in –
You've got the job as bidie-in.

Hamish Whyte

14

Great Western Road

Glasgow, you look beatific in blue
and I've a Saturday before me
for galleries and poems,
a house full of Haydn,
and beneath my kitchen window,
tennis stars in saris
lobbing backhands at the bins.
French coffee, and who knows maybe
Allen Ginsberg in my bath!
then round to the dairy
where scones are cooling on the rack
and Jimmy won't let me leave
till I've tried one there and then,
here, where the new Glasgow started –
an old grey city going blonde
whose Asian shops are full of fruits
we owe to Cap'n Bligh
and I'm so juiced I could walk clear
to Loch Lomond,
past busses stripping the willow
all along Great Western Road
but I just browse bargains in banjos
and pop-art knitted ties,
before checking out the crime section
at Caledonia Books,
finding Friesias in the flowershops
and in the second hand record store,

Bruckner's Third,
The Cleveland
under Szell:
so sad; like falling for passing students
with that black haired, blue eyed look,
or buying basil and chorizos . . .
In the afternoon I'll look at paintings
in Dougie Thomson's Mayfest show,
maybe stroll down to the studio
to view some archive film,
past the motorways and multi-storeys
of Grieve's Ultimate Cowcaddens,
the peeling pawn at George's Cross
where, today, everything is redeemable
because tonight there'll be guitar poets
from Russia at the Third Eye Centre.
And later I'll cook zarzuela
for a new and nimble friend.
God Glasgow it's glorious
just to gulp you down in heartfuls,
feeling something quite like love.

Donny O'Rourke

15

Midge

The evening is perfect, my sisters.
The loch lies silent, the air is still.
The sun's last rays linger over the water
and there is a faint smirr, almost a smudge
of summer rain. Sisters, I smell supper,
and what is more perfect than supper?
It is emerging from the wood,
in twos and threes, a dozen in all,
making such a chatter and a clatter
as it reaches the rocky shore,
admiring the arrangements of the light.
See the innocents, my sisters,
the clumsy ones, the laughing ones,
the rolled-up sleeves and the flapping shorts,
there is even a kilt (god of the midges,
you are good to us!). So gather your forces,
leave your tree-trunks, forsake the rushes,
fly up from the sour brown mosses
to the sweet flesh of face and forearm.
Think of your eggs. What does the egg need?
Blood, and blood. Blood is what the egg needs.
Our men have done their bit, they've gone,
it was all they were good for, poor dears. Now
it is up to us. The egg is quietly screaming
for supper, blood, supper, blood, supper!
Attack, my little Draculas, my Amazons!
Look at those flailing arms and stamping feet.

They're running, swatting, swearing, oh they're hopeless.
Keep at them, ladies. This is a feast.
This is a midsummer night's dream.
Soon we shall all lie down filled and rich,
and lay, and lay, and lay, and lay, and lay.

Edwin Morgan

16

The Lighthouse

As good a climb as any, now the day's near done
      the hill ahent the bothy –
a dry burn, then a basalt knuckle
like a throne,
      should you care to queen it
among shivery bracken
      a wheen grazing sheep.

Already the Western Isles
lie dusty-pink along the horizon,
      and like a prodigal in a nightclub,
the Scalpay lighthouse
      keeps flashing its signature

three-white-every-twenty-second beam.

Kathleen Jamie

17

O Waly, Waly

O waly, waly up the bank!
  And waly, waly, down the brae!
And waly, waly yon burn-side,
  Where I and my love wont to gae!

I lean'd my back unto an aik,
  I thought it was a trusty tree,
But first it bow'd, and syne it brak,
  Sae my true-love did lightly me.

O waly, waly! but love be bony
  A little time, while it is new,
But when 'tis auld, it waxeth cauld,
  And fades away like morning dew.

O wherefore should I busk my head?
  Or wherefore should I kame my hair?
For my true-love has me forsook,
  And says he'll never love me mair.

Now Arthur-Seat shall be my bed,
  The sheets shall ne'er be fyl'd by me,
Saint Anton's well shall be my drink,
  Since my true-love has forsaken me.

Anon.

18

Bed in Summer

In winter I get up at night
And dress by yellow candle-light.
In summer, quite the other way,
I have to go to bed by day.

I have to go to bed and see
The birds still hopping on the tree,
Or hear the grown-up people's feet
Still going past me in the street.

And does it not seem hard to you,
When all the sky is clear and blue,
And I should like so much to play
To have to go to bed by day?

Robert Louis Stevenson

19

'One Renfrewshire Man to Another'

W.S.G.

To articulate clearly what is difficult to say
I shall transmit this by a beam from a lighthouse
Over the eventful, unforgiving waters
Across many a headland and many a bay.

Douglas Dunn

20

A Galloway Burn in June

Brown burn water dropping
  Between the grey stones,
The lapse and the murmur,
  The bright overtones
Of cuckoo and curlew
  And faraway trill
Of a lark; great blue shadows
  Stride over the hill:
Breeze and bird-call are blended
  With murmur of bees;
Sun and wind stroke the grasses
  And finger the trees.
Is it sunlight or greenlight?
  This shimmer of leaves;
Is it seeing or dreaming,
  The dapple that weaves
Across the brown water
  That murmurs and spills
Through the grey stones forever
  Among the green hills?

Dorothy Margaret Paulin

21

The Lost Word

I am on the tip of your tongue,
hidden in the creases of your memory.
I am disobedient,
I will not come when called.
I feel your jaw clench.
I tremble slightly
when you umm and urr
but I lurk just out of reach.

I am exactly what you need
to answer a question
or win an argument.
I lie curled in the dictionary
sound asleep.
You cannot find my starting letter
to begin your search.
I am most precious to you
when you fight to remember me.

Then, without warning,
days or hours later
I appear.
I pop into your head —
a snail's pace Superman
too late to save the world.
You're so surprised
you blurt me out.

That's it, you think
the word I wanted!
And everyone stares at you
like you've gone mad.
But for once they're listening
just to me,
loud and clear and strong.

Not part of a longer sentence
but me,
by myself
alone.
And I feel . . .
    . . . and I feel . . .
        . . . I feel urr . . .
            . . . feel umm . . .
                . . . urrrr ummm
                . . .
You know . . .
    . . . really umm . . .
        . . . really urr . . .
Well . . .
like *that* anyway.

Lindsay MacRae

22

Amazing Grace

Amazing grace, how sweet the sound
That saved a wretch like me.
I once was lost, but now I'm found;
Was blind, but now I see.

'Twas grace that taught my heart to fear
And grace my fear relieved.
How precious did that grace appear
The hour I first believed.

Through many dangers, toils and snares,
We have already come.
'Twas grace that brought us safe thus far,
And grace will lead us home.

When we've been there ten thousand years,
Bright shining as the sun,
We've no less days to sing God's praise
Than when we first begun.

John Newton

23

The Mermaid Sat on the Carlin Stane

The mermaid sat on the Carlin stane,
A-kaimin her gowden hair,
The may ne'er was in Clydesdale wide
Was ever hauf sae fair.

Anon.

24

from The Bruce

A! Fredome is a noble thing
Fredome mays man to haiff liking.
Fredome all solace to man giffis,
He levys at es that frely levys.
A noble hart may haiff nane es
Na ellys nocht that may him ples
Gyff fredome failyhe, for fre liking
Is yharnt our all other thing.
Na he that ay has levyt fre
May nocht knaw weill the propyrté
The angyr na the wrechyt dome
That is couplt to foule thyrldome,
Bot gyff he had assayit it.
Than all perquer he suld it wyt,
And suld think fredome mar to prys
Than all the gold in warld that is.

John Barbour,
translated by A. A. M. Duncan

25

The Roadside Lined with Ragweed, the Sharp Hills

The roadside lined with ragweed, the sharp hills
    Standing against the glow of eve, the patch
Of rough white oats 'mongst darkling granite knolls,
    The ferny coverts where the adders hatch,
The hollow that the northern sea upfills,
    The seagull wheeling by with strange, sad calls,
All these, this evening, weary me. Full fain
    Would I turn up the little elm tree way
And under the last elm tree, once again
    Stretch myself with my head among the grass;
    So lying, tyne the memories of day
    And let my loosed, insatiate being pass
Into the blackbird's song of summer ease,
Or, with the white moon, rise in spirit from the trees.

Robert Louis Stevenson

26

Nine Haiku for Esther Inglis

Born France 1571; moved to Scotland in early childhood,
daughter of Huguenot refugees; lived most of her life in Leith
Edinburgh, where she died in poverty, 1624; considered by King
James VI of Scotland (I of England) to be the finest calligrapher
in the land; also an embroiderer and miniaturist portrait
painter.

Goose and crow quills scratch
a tiny patch of parchment,
giving flight to words.

I paint myself – not
vanity, necessity:
a lord may hire me.

A ragged man sells
seed pearls from a burn; I stitch
them to books for kings.

Honeysuckle scrolls,
thistle spikes and fleur-de-lis
twine with damask rose.

Like a butterfly,
I inhale from harebell cups
the tang of blue ink.

I was King Jamie's
'most exquisite writer in
this realm'. Now debt stalks.

My constant husband,
dear daughters and son, I fear
my steady hand fails.

From the Lord goodness,
from myself nothing. Till death
I will chart his praise.

All creation dwells
in a leaf, bird, bloom or word
in my Maker's book.

Gerda Stevenson

27

Looking for Scotland

The rolling field
waved, brown over the bright
hedges. Her colander
burned with the fruit,
gooseberries, a few red,
to give a green jam
mixed with elderflower.
Brunton Turret
was not far away.
The white and brimming miles
of Roman Wall,
the North Tyne river.
How far away?
A mere ten years,
yet in those ten
how many muses
came and died?
Putting sugar to fruit
she still walks strong,
though her friends perished
and her friends' loves have gone.
She left the slopes
of black-ripe legend
for the feared country
it barred out.
Her friends' muses perished,
year upon year of jam

scattered with elder florets
were consumed like rhyme,
yet the memory of it
fell like fruit in time,
like bush and hedgerow fruit
she rolled, rich as the past,
rich as what perishes
into the bladed field
and does not come again,
no, does not come again
until the earth is worked
and stores of song may spring.

Sally Evanz

28

Timetable

We all remember school, of course:
the lino warming, shoe bag smell, expanse
of polished floor. It's where we learned
to wait: hot cheeked in class, dreaming,
bored, for cheesy milk, for noisy now.
We learned to count, to rule off days,
and pattern time in coloured squares:
purple English, dark green Maths.

We hear the bells, sometimes,
for years, the squeal and crack
of chalk on black. We walk, don't run,
in awkward pairs, hoping for the open door,
a foreign teacher, fire drill. And love
is long aertex summers, tennis sweat,
and somewhere, someone singing flat.
The art room, empty, full of light.

Kate Clanchy

29

Blake's Wife

My love walked in a wild domain
I followed him as best I could
beyond the boundaries of the brain
half credible, half understood.
He hardly slept, strange music played
he wrote, dreamed, painted.

In love I pitied, helped him work
on copper plates, the ink and fire.
We cooled it down in printed books
of prophecy or soul's desire.
'The lark an angel on the wing'
purest line engraving.

His *spectre* visited for days
and silent brooded on the house.
I waited, made his soup, his clothes
until he found a form in chaos.
I gathered fragments he had scattered:
Job, Dante, Milton uttered.

I rocked no babies at the breast:
this child I had was child enough.
Like Mary I was chosen, blessed
to bear this spirit through his life.
'Jerusalem in every man'
this grain of sand in Albion.

My love walked in a wild domain
I followed him as best I could
beyond the boundaries of the brain
half credible, half understood.
We turned our trials into art
hammered the work upon the heart.

Tessa Ransford

30

On being observed

When I woke up she asked me what I'd been smiling at
as I slept. Was it dachshunds? she said. No, I replied
I'm pretty sure it was a dream about organisational change
at work. The treads of the steps to our office grew narrower
and we all had to wear smaller shoes. But the smiling?
she asked. Oh, I was probably just being polite.

Vicki Husband

July

Changed

For months he taught us, stiff-faced.
His old tweed jacket closely buttoned up,
his gestures careful and deliberate.

We didn't understand what he was teaching us.
It was as if a veil, a gauzy bandage, got between
what he was showing us and what we thought we saw.

He had the air of a gardener, fussily protective
of young seedlings, but we couldn't tell
if he was hiding something or we simply couldn't see it.

At first we noticed there were often scraps of leaves
on the floor where he had stood. Later, thin wisps
of thread like spider's web fell from his jacket.

Finally we grew to understand the work. And on that day
he opened his jacket, which to our surprise
seemed lined with patterned fabric of many shimmering hues.

Then he smiled and sighed. And with this movement
the lining rippled and instantly the room was filled
with a flickering storm of swirling butterflies.

Dave Calder

2

Seal, River Clyde

Flourishing, aye, its glass filled with dazzle
all the way up to the sky, *Glas-cu* greened
as if St Mungo has just passed by. It might
have been just yesterday he broke a branch
off a tree and it burst into flame
and could this be the tree, could this be the tree?

Out of the tree a robin sang
its last song into the exhausted air,
but St Mungo was there to pick it up
off the road in case the buses killed it again,
breathing into its mouth, saving its name
and could this be the bird, could this be the bird?

Under Jamaica Bridge, a log rolls and turns
into a shining seal. It has swum past the armadillo,
past Glasgow's glass eyes, snakes of children
in high-vis, to search for the live thing
in the water, the salmon that swallowed a ring
and could this be the fish, could this be the fish?

The seal looks at the children and they look back
as if they have a question to ask before the tree
comes alight on the banks of the Clyde, where
the salmon swims to the mouth of the seal
who has something to tell before the bell tolls
and could this be the bell, could this be the bell?

Imtiaz Dharker

3

July Evening

A bird's voice chinks and tinkles
Alone in the gaunt reedbed –
 Tiny silversmith
Working late in the evening.

I sit and listen. The rooftop
With a quill of smoke stuck in it
 Wavers against the sky
In the dreamy heat of summer.

Flowers' closing time: bee lurches
Across the hayfield, singing
 And feeling its drunken way
Round the air's invisible corners.

And grass is grace. And charlock
Is gold of its own bounty.
 The broken chair by the wall
Is one with immortal landscapes.

Something has been completed
That everything is part of,
 Something that will go on
Being completed forever.

Norman MacCaig

4

The Two Sisters

There were twa sisters lived in a bower
    Binnorie, O Binnorie!
There came a knicht to be their wooer,
    By the bonnie mill-dams of Binnorie.

He courted the eldest with glove and ring;
But he loved the youngest aboon a' thing.

He courted the eldest with brooch and knife;
But he loved the youngest as his life.

The eldest she was vexèd sair,
And sair envied her sister fair.

Intil her bow'r she cou'dna rest;
With grief and spite she almus brast.

Upon a mornin' fair and clear,
She cried upon her sister dear:

'Oh, sister! come to the sea-strand,
And see our father's ships come to land.'

She's ta'en her by the milk-white hand,
And lad her down to yon sea-strand.

The youngest stood upon a stane,
The eldest came and pushed her in.

She took her by the middle sma',
And dash'd her bonnie back to the jaw.

'O sister, sister, reach your hand,
And ye shall be heir of half my land.'

'O sister, I'll not reach my hand,
And I'll be heir of all your land.'

'O sister, reach me but your glove,
And sweet William shall be your love.'

'Sink on, nor hope for hand or glove,
And sweet William shall better be my love.

'Your cherry cheeks, and your yellow hair,
Gar'd me gang maiden evermair.'

Sometimes she sunk, sometimes she swam,
Until she came to the miller's dam.

Oh, out it came the miller's son,
And saw the fair maid floating down.

'O father, father, draw your dam
  Binnorie, O Binnorie!
There's a mermaid or a milk-white swan
  In the bonnie mill-dams of Binnorie.'

The miller quickly drew the dam,
and there he found a drowned woman.

You cou'dna see her yellow hair,
For gowd and pearl that were so rare.

You cou'dna see her middle sma',
For her gowden girdle sae braw.

You cou'dna see her fingers white,
For gowden rings that were sae bright.

By there came a harper fine,
That harpèd to the king at dine.

And when he lookt that ladye on,
He sighed, and made a heavy moan.

He made a harp of her breast-bone,
Whose sounds would melt a heart of stone.

He's ta'en three locks of her yellow hair,
And with them strung his harp sae fair.

He brought the harp to her father's hall;
And there was the court assembled all.

He laid the harp upon a stane,
And straight it began to play alane.

'Oh, yonder sits my father, the king,
And yonder sits my mother, the queen.

But the last tune that the harp played then,
Was – 'Woe to my sister, false Helen!'

Anon.

5

Flowers and Trees

Boon nature scattered, free and wild,
Each plant or flower, the mountain's child.
Here eglantine embalmed the air,
Hawthorn and hazel mingled there;
The primrose pale, and violet flower,
Found in such cliff a narrow bower;
Fox-glove and night-shade, side by side,
Emblems of punishment and pride,
Grouped their dark hues with every stain
The weather-beaten crags retain.
With boughs that quaked at every breath,
Grey birch and aspen wept beneath;
Aloft, the ash and warrior oak
Cast anchor in the rifted rock;
And, higher yet, the pine-tree hung
His shattered trunk, and frequent flung,
Where seemed the cliffs to meet on high,
His boughs athwart the narrowed sky.
Highest of all, where white peaks glanced,
Where glistening streamers waved and danced.
The wanderer's eye could barely view
The summer heaven's delicious blue;
So wonderous wild, the whole might seem
The scenery of a fairy dream.

Sir Walter Scott

6

Blue Bonnets over the Border

March, march, Ettrick and Teviotdale,
Why the deil dinna ye march forward in order?
March, march, Eskdale and Liddesdale,
All the Blue Bonnets are bound for the Border.
    Many a banner spread
    Flutters above your head,
Many a crest that is famous in story.
    Mount and make ready then,
    Sons of the mountain glen,
Fight for the Queen and the old Scottish glory.

Come from the hills where your hirsels are grazing,
Come from the glen of the buck and the roe;
Come to the crag where the beacon is blazing,
Come with the buckler, the lance, and the bow.
    Trumpets are sounding,
    War-steeds are bounding,
Stand to your arms then, and march in good order;
    England shall many a day
    Tell of the bloody fray,
When the Blue Bonnets came over the Border.

Sir Walter Scott

7

Standing by Thistles

It's not the beauty of the hill
binds us on this path
by sedge and thistle, such a small path
stony, sharp; a path for
short encounters, yet we stand
and stand
breathless in the summer rain

Anne MacLeod

8

Carpe Diem

From my study window
        I see you
below in the garden, a hand
        here pruning
or leaning across to snip
        a wayward shoot,

a daub of powder-blue in a
        profusion of green;
then next moment, you are
        no longer there –
only to reappear, this time
        perfectly framed

in dappling sunlight, with
        an armful of ivy
you've trimmed, topped by
        hyacinth blooms,
fragrant survivors of last
        night's frost.

And my heart misses a beat
        at love for you,
knowing a time will come
        when you are
no longer there, nor I here
        to watch you

on a day of such simplicity.
Meantime let us
make sure we clasp each
shared moment
in cupped hands, like water
we dare not spill.

Stewart Conn

9

What I Remember

is not the race itself but the evening
which disappeared in a tangle of diving
sunlight and nerves as I hugged myself,
chilled, and waited for the starter, bent
forward, the tang of mown grass
sprayed like water and the white lines
freshly painted on the spongy red track,
breasting the tape, alone and splendid,
queen of my own universe, then the medal
like a tiny sun catching the last of the light,
and feeling as if my heart would burst.

Tracey Herd

10

Annie Laurie

Maxwellton braes are bonnie,
Where early fa's the dew,
And it's there that Annie Laurie
Gie'd me her promise true;
Gie'd me her promise true,
That ne'er forgot shall be;
But for bonnie Annie Laurie
I'd lay doun my head and dee.

Her brow is like the snaw-drift,
Her neck is like the swan,
Her face it is the fairest
That e'er the sun shone on;
That e'er the sun shone on,
And dark blue is her e'e;
And for bonnie Annie Laurie
I'd lay doun my head and dee.

Like dew on the gowan lying
Is the fa' o' her fairy feet;
And like winds in summer sighing
Her voice is low and sweet;
Her voice is low and sweet
And she's a' the world to me,
And for bonnie Annie Laurie
I'd lay doun my head and dee.

Alicia Ann, Lady John Scott

11

Six pomegranate seeds

They burst on my tongue,
those seeds, when I ate them
one by one,

the taste of the world I remembered,
the colour of gardens
before I threw away the sun.

Imtiaz Dharker

12

Windowbox

I sowed nightscented stocks with the halfgrown hope
that this was more like gardening
than impatiens in pots.

They grew anaemic and spindly
coated by dust from the street.
From the ground they looked like weeds.

Nothing flashy or flowery
like a trumpetting hippaestrum
or a petal drenched Black-eyed Susan

and even I who planted them
rarely thought to look out
except maybe in the evenings

when the cool damp of Summer rain
sweated in the air
like an extra sense

and the night scent swam in
clear as spearmint
and soothed away the city noise.

Then there grew a garden:
rosebeds and herbs,
tangles of scarlet runners.

Angela McSeveney

13

Foreign Lands

Up into the cherry tree
Who should climb but little me?
I held the trunk with both my hands
And looked abroad on foreign lands.

I saw the next door garden lie,
Adorned with flowers, before my eye,
And many pleasant places more
That I had never seen before.

I saw the dimpling river pass
And be the sky's blue looking-glass;
The dusty roads go up and down
With people tramping in to town.

If I could find a higher tree
Farther and farther I should see,
To where the grown-up river slips
Into the sea among the ships,

To where the roads on either hand
Lead onward into fairy land,
Where all the children dine at five,
And all the playthings come alive.

Robert Louis Stevenson

14

The Blues

The lights are on all over Hamilton.
The sky is dark, blue
as a stained glass window in an unfrequented church
say, by Chagall, with grand and glorious chinks
of pinks and purples,
glittering jewels on those glass fronted buildings
where the lifts are all descending
and the doors are
being closed.
                    You're out there somewhere,
going to a concert in wide company or maybe
sitting somewhere weaving a carpet
like a giant tapestry, coloured grey,
pale brown, weaving the wool
back in at the edges of the frame, your
fingers deft as they turn the wool in tight and
gentle curves.
                    Or somewhere else.
                    What do I do
                    except imagine you?
                    The river I keep crossing
                    keeps going north. The trains
                    in the night cross it too.
                    Their silver carriages are blue.

Alan Riach

15

Scottish rain

Gets in yer neb, lugs,
unner thi oxters tae.
Oan yer heid, in yer een
til ye're drookit, ken?

An it's aye cauld
an gaes sidie-ways.
Whit, warm rain?
Nae here (mebbe in Spain).

Woke up this mornin,
crawled oot o bed,
keeked oot thi windae pane
Aw naw! Rainin again!

Tom Bryan

16

Hosai

A' sealltainn air ais air an tràigh,
Fiù's làrach mo chois' air falbh.

Rody Gorman

Hosai

Looking back at the beach,
even my footprints
have disappeared.

Rody Gorman

17

Peat Cutting

And we left our beds in the dark
And we drove a cart to the hill
And we buried the jar of ale in the bog
And our small blades glittered in the dayspring
And we tore dark squares, thick pages
From the Book of Fire
And we spread them wet on the heather
And horseflies, poisonous hooks,
Stuck in our arms
And we laid off our coats
And our blades sank deep into water
And the lord of the bog, the kestrel
Paced round the sun
And at noon we leaned on our tuskars
– The cold unburied jar
Touched, like a girl, a circle of burning mouths
And the boy found a wild bees' comb
And his mouth was a sudden brightness
And the kestrel fell
And a lark flashed a needle across the west
And we spread a thousand peats
Between one summer star
And the black chaos of fire at the earth's centre.

George Mackay Brown

18

Dazzledance

I have an eye of silver,
I have an eye of gold,
I have a tongue of reed-grass
   and a story to be told.

I have a hand of metal,
I have a hand of clay,
I have two arms of granite
   and a song for every day.

I have a foot of damson,
I have a foot of corn,
I have two legs of leaf-stalk
   and a dance for every morn.

I have a dream of water,
I have a dream of snow,
I have a thought of wildfire
   and a harp-string long and low.

I have an eye of silver,
I have an eye of gold,
I have a tongue of reed-grass
   and a story to be told.

John Rice

19

Teneu

Also known as Saint Enoch, 6th century, probably pagan,
later claimed as a Christian saint; mother of the City of
Glasgow, and of Saint Mungo / Kentigern.

'Teneu!' His owl call rang from the Mother Rock – 'Teneu!'
I slipped from bed, past my father's door, rising dew
a spur at my heels, up to the whale-back summit
and our tryst: Owain, my chosen one, quite
the part in his sister's borrowed gown, curve of calf
a moonlit glimmer through a frayed seam – 'It snagged
on the rampart,' he whispered, following my hungry eye.

We slid into the Maiden Stone cleft, a perfect fit –
tender his breath, 'Teneu,' he sighed,
nuzzling my flesh below the stars.

Rowans ripen on the branch; my belly grows full;
'Teneu!' my father's wolf howl splits the air,
'For this you'll pay!' I'm whipped, and lashed
to a chariot – a death trap with no horse –
wheels rumble under my back, and gather speed
as black clouds roll; then silence; I fly
over Dunpelder's ramparts, my babe
floating under my heart – hang
on the air with a prayer to Coventina:
Hold safe this life in my womb's well.

She hears, and offers up her hidden spring,
its deep green sphagnum cloak to break our fall.
The land lies still. A hawk calls. The ropes
have slackened. I rise and walk, two hearts
drumming through my blood.

'Teneu!' My father's fear is greater now
than all his rage – his adder tongue flicks
my name, 'Teneu! I know you for a witch!
You will not live to spawn that child –
I'll have you drowned!'

We bob, spin, plunge and soar
on a million hissing knives, no oar
for guide, a doll inside a doll
inside a skin and willow shell;
Oh, Coventina, quell these waves
within and all about me,
cradle me safe to shore!

I sweat on cool sand, my mind a haze
in the dawn haar; I dream of an oak
that never grew, a red-breasted bird
that never flew, a ring in a fish
that never swam, and a swaying bell
that never rang.

The haar lifts. Sticks crackle and blaze.
A stranger tends the fire, and holds a cross
to my brow; I heave in time with the tide
that carried me here, ebbing now, gasp
my name to this man whose hand I grip
in the last arc of birthing pain: *Teneu!*

Gerda Stevenson

Note: Glasgow's coat of arms, linked to legends of Teneu's son, Saint Mungo, is
associated with the rhyme: 'Here is the bird that never flew, Here is the tree that
never grew, Here is the bell that never rang, Here is the fish that never swam.'

20

The Only Bloody Hill in Scotland

Ten summers young. The day, all heat on heather.
The purple pathway brittle underfoot,
The peat as springy's cork,
I clambered Lochnagar for the first time,
By Allt-na-Guibhsaich, startling a grouse.
My birthday, and my father's gift, the climb.

'Scotland's a pocket-hanky from the top. Dee's source and
    Don's
You'll see,' said he, all merriment, all cheer.
My sandals slithered, slipping on the shale.
The sun raised crops of freckles on his brow, and queer
And lovely clouds sailed silent by
My widening eye, mysterious as swans.

Suddenly, gaunt and gashed into the sky it soared
High as a bird, a grey bird rising far,
Wings bent against the wind in that massif
The darkling, stark motif of Lochnagar.

My father had not lied: like tents below,
Dwarfed tiny hills were pinned and fixed to heath
With Lochnagar, the general. They, his guards, beneath.

Three climbers died that day.
Fate flicked them off the crags like fragile wrens
Dropped from their lofty perch.

Happily tramping home, we passed the search
For that doomed trio. So, I learned the Gods
Are cruel to those mortals they don't love.
It ill behoves to anger those above.

At sixteen summers, gauche, with beau in tow
(Sunday, Hell's Angel. Weekdays, city clerk)
I scaled the Fox's Ladder. Halfway up
We stopped to drink cheap whisky from a cup.
I sang Lord Byron's song. Sank to the heather
And nuzzled naked moss like any lover.
My dull companion fretted, pining for
Bike, sandwiches, the football match he'd missed;
He liked to do his courting in the park
Clothes buttoned to the neck, where all was dark.
And, like a sheep that's never left the pen,
Found freedom frightening. He didn't come again.

A cargo train, at thirty I was back,
Laden with rucksacks, offspring trailing slow.
It was a vital matter they should know
This family member, icon, lover, shrine,
Boers' trek their Laocoon struggle past each pine
Tumbling and stumbling like loosened scree:
'We want a rest! A piece! A drink! A pee!'
Half-dragged, cajoled, unsteady candles guttering,
Their sire, a travelled mountaineer, muttering,
'I've climbed Mont Blanc. This mountain's just a pimple.
It's not the only bloody hill in Scotland.
You climb it every year, like some weird ritual.'

Forty. Marriage over. Kids half grown
I climbed the serpent, silver way alone,
And then it rained! Sweet waters bathed my face
The benison of that beloved place!
The winds that rained sharks' teeth across the tarn,
That shook the doors on cursing crofter's barn
Blew tatters of misogamy away,
Built arcs of rainbows, gleams across the grey.
Mountain of my delight, of all my knowings,
Your memory's a field of many sowings!

At fifty, with a Munro-bagging son,
I took Dod Byron's route by Invercauld.
'It's far. The heather's deep. You're none too *fit*,' he said
And like a faithful collie raced ahead,
Before. Then, sat and waited. Lit a fag,
A pencil line that smudged with every drag.
While up the tortoise slope, jaw set, face white,
Legs like cement, each steepening step a fight,
I toiled. He said, 'Quite soon the day will come
When this will be beyond you.' Dearest son,
When the time comes I cannot touch the skies
I'd like a bullet, straight between the eyes!

Sheena Blackhall

21

Soondscapes

I da dizzied hoose, a strum of flechs baet
endless drums fornenst a frenzied window.
Belligerent, dey want nedder in nor oot.

Apö da broo, ahint a wheeshtit chapel,
twa windmills spin new soondscapes owre
da laand, kert-wheelin alleluias.

Cloistert granite hadds a orchestration
o birds, a oorie whirr, a vimmerin
o whaaps an peewits. Da wind

troo da grind is a spaekin in tongues
wi da bruckit feed-hoop tunin in:
idder-wirdly, intimately insistent.

Aa dis music ta lö tae, ta slip inta:
a aald organ nönin, a hushie hubbelskyu.
Up owre da hill, airms turn, da haert lifts.

Christine De Luca

Soundscapes

In the dizzied house, a strum o flies beat
endless drums against a frenzied window.
Belligerent, they want neither in nor out.

On the brow of the hill, behind a silent chapel,
two windmills spin new soundscapes over
the land, cart-wheeling alleluias.

Cloistered granite holds an orchestration
of birds, an eerie whirr, tremulous sounds
of curlew and lapwing. The wind

through the metal gate is a speaking in tongues
with the broken feed-hoop tuning in:
other-worldly, intimately insistent.

All this music to attend to, to slip into:
an old organ droning, an uproarious lullaby.
Up over da hill, arms turn, the heart lifts.

Christine De Luca

22

Haunfast

Somethin auld: the years afore
Somethin new: the morn's door
Somethin borraed: kirk, or haa
Somethin blue: sky clear o sna
As bricht as ony wattergaw
A cloodless future spent as twa

Sheena Blackhall

23

Turner Prize

A coo an a cauf
Cut in hauf.

William Hershaw

24

Welcome Wee One

O ma darlin wee one
At last you are here in the wurld
And wi' aa your wisdom
Your een bricht as the stars,
You've filled this hoose with licht,
Yer trusty wee haun, your globe o' a heid,
My cherished yin, my hert's ain!

O ma darlin wee one
The hale wurld welcomes ye:
The mune glowes; the hearth wairms.
Let your life hae luck, health, charm,
Ye are my bonny blessed bairn,
My small miraculous gift.
I never kent luve like this.

Jackie Kay

25

The Song of the Grasshopper

First of all, it is their songs
That she listens for, the dry chirr
Of thigh against thigh, the dead give-away
As to where they are hiding, serenading
Each other in the knee-high grass.

Bent over double, or on all-fours,
She tracks them down with the diligence
Of bloodhounds, and then, to my amazement,
Pounces, and they are hers. Then, slowly,
She opens her hands and begins to sing.

And the wonder of it is, that they
Stand in her palms and listen. As if her
Song was their reward for her four year-old
Rough-handling. As her voice trails off,
The grasshoppers become their names,

And disappear.

Gordon Meade

26

Boat Song

'Hail to the chief who in triumph advances!
   Honoured and blessed be the evergreen Pine!
Long may the tree, in his banner that glances,
   Flourish, the shelter and grace of our line!
     Heaven send it happy dew,
     Earth lend it sap anew,
Gayly to bourgeon, and broadly to grow,
     While every Highland glen
     Sends our shout back agen,
Roderigh Vich Alpine, dhu, ho! ieroe!

'Ours is no sapling, chance-sown by the fountain,
   Blooming at Beltane, in winter to fade;
When the whirlwind has stripped every leaf on the
   mountain,
   The more shall Clan-Alpine exult in her shade.
     Moored in the rifted rock,
     Proof to the tempest's shock,
Firmer he roots him the ruder it blow;
     Menteith and Breadalbane, then,
     Echo his praise agen,
Roderigh Vich Alpine dhu, ho! ieroe!

'Proudly our pibroch has thrilled in Glen Fruin,
  And Bannochar's groans to our slogan replied;
Glen Luss and Ross-dhu, they are smoking in ruin,
  And the best of Loch Lomond lie dead on her side.
    Widow and Saxon maid
    Long shall lament our raid,
Think of Clan-Alpine with fear and with woe;
    Lennox and Leven-glen
    Shake when they hear agen,
Roderigh Vich Alpine dhu, ho! ieroe!

'Row, vassals, row, for the pride of the Highlands!
  Stretch to your oars, for the evergreen Pine!
O! that the rose-bud that graces yon islands
  Were wreathed in a garland around him to twine!
    O that some seedling gem,
    Worthy such noble stem,
Honoured and blessed in their shadow might grow!
    Loud should Clan-Alpine then
    Ring from her deepmost glen,
Roderigh Vich Alpine dhu, ho! ieroe!'

                                        Sir Walter Scott

27

Songs of the Scottish Exam Board English Marker

I.

The High Schools, Academies, Colleges, Saints,
I shuffle them between my hands.

Morgan, Madras, Kelvinside, Wester Hailes,
I red ink their mistakes.

Dalbeattie, Lochgelly, Our Lady's, Balfron,
I envelope, number and grade.

Selkirk, Dalziel, Balweary, Nairn,
I process their thoughts, dreams and lives.

So many lives pass before my eyes
on the way to the rest of theirs
while mine stops here with this slow and painful
    business.

Through the small glass square in my attic roof
the sound of children's laughter in the street
upsets my penning rhythm.

I lift up my head in the summer heat then,
Hazelhead, Sandwick, St Columba's, Arbroath,
Royal High, Bannockburn, Dalkeith.

II.

No future 'A' pass Higher here:
she wrote of her father and feelings,
how he lay on a waterbed
whey-faced and skeletal from fighting the cancer
the last time her mother had taken her
to the hospice for the dying.

I wrote on it:
gives a clear account of a personal experience;
communicates a sense of involvement;
sentences accurate but not varied;
does not demonstrate skill with language
or overall distinction of Credit English;
General, Grade 3.

O God,
when my final examination comes,
do not measure me
by the same pitiless criteria.

William Hershaw

28

'Columbine' Cameron

Jean Cameron – also known as Jenny – born Glen Dessary,
Knoydart, c.1695, died East Kilbride, 1772, where a memorial has
been erected to her memory; heroine of the 1745 Jacobite rising.

I look North to Glen Dessary –
home – though can't return
to its devastation, always North,
to the 'Glen of the South-facing place',
my back turned on those false tales
that fanned about me like redcoat wildfire,
growing flanks, battalions of lies
sweeping over the border, on and on
(never falling back, as we did at Derby),
gathering heat till they licked the heels
of Fleet Street, and danced in the footlights
of Drury Lane – a play named after me,
would you believe! *Columbine Cameron*,
Britannia's nemesis, sprite of hell,
nightly rousing rebellion
in Scotia's frozen wastes –
such was the reach of my fame,
in this high-stakes game of war;
it seems our masters need a whore,
a bitch to blame – and better still
if she has 'the vulgar Highland tongue',
a 'she-cavalier' with claymore.

I've become in others' eyes
so many versions, all perversions
of my self. But there's none
among them can tarnish the truth
of that August day on summer's cusp,
leaves turning to gold by the shores of Loch Shiel:
I led my clan to Glenfinnan – three hundred men –
our hope with the Standard rising high.

Gerda Stevenson

29

Coronach

He is gone on the mountain,
  He is lost to the forest,
Like a summer-dried fountain,
  When our need was the sorest.
The font, reappearing,
  From the rain-drops shall borrow,
But to us comes no cheering,
  To Duncan no morrow!

The hand of the reaper
  Takes the ears that are hoary,
But the voice of the weeper
  Wails manhood in glory.
The autumn winds rushing
  Waft the leaves that are searest,
But our flower was in flushing,
  When blighting was nearest.

Fleet foot on the corrie,
  Sage counsel in cumber,
Red hand in the foray,
  How sound is thy slumber!
Like the dew on the mountain,
  Like the foam on the river,
Like the bubble on the fountain,
  Thou art gone, and for ever!

Sir Walter Scott

Lanarkshire Girls

Coming into Glasgow
in our red bus through those green fields. And
Summer annoyed us thrusting
leafy branches through the upstairs windows.
Like a boy with a stick through railings,
rattling us. We bent whole treetops
squeezing through and they rained down twigs, broken
bits of foliage, old blossom on the roof,
chucked hard wee balls of unripe fruit,
drumming us out of the country.

Then it was
shabby schemes, gospel halls, chapels, Orange halls,
doctors' surgeries, the crematorium, the zoo,
gap sites where August already frittered the stuffing out of
unpurpling fireweed and splintering thistles
till the blank blue sky was dot-dot-dotted
with whiskery asterisks.

Soon the coherent cliffs of Tollcross,
the many mansions of those lovely red and
blackened tenements. Our country bus sped
past the city stops, the women in their
slippers at the doors of dairies,
the proud pubs on every corner, accelerated
along the glamorous Gallowgate, juddered by
Reeta's gallus fashions and the
gorgeous dragons of Terry Tattoo Artist, till it
spilled us out, fourteen years old, dreaming ourselves up,
with holiday money burning a hole in our pockets
at the corner of Jamaica Street.

Liz Lochhead

31

Sounds of the Day

When a clatter came,
it was horses crossing the ford.
When the air creaked, it was
a lapwing seeing us off the premises
of its private marsh. A snuffling puff
ten yards from the boat was the tide blocking and
unblocking a hole in a rock.
When the black drums rolled, it was water
falling sixty feet into itself.

When the door
scraped shut, it was the end
of all the sounds there are.

You left me
beside the quietest fire in the world.

I thought I was hurt in my pride only,
forgetting that,
when you plunge your hand in freezing water,
you feel
a bangle of ice round your wrist
before the whole hand goes numb.

Norman MacCaig

August

I

Corn Rigs

It was upon a Lammas night,
  When corn rigs are bonie,
Beneath the moon's unclouded light
  I held awa to Annie:
The time flew by, wi' tentless heed,
  Till 'tween the late and early;
Wi' sma' persuasion she agreed,
  To see me thro' the barley.

  Corn rigs, ah barley rigs,
    An' corn rigs are bonie:
  O, I'll ne'er forget that happy night,
    Amang the rigs wi' Annie.

The sky was blue, the wind was still,
  The moon was shining clearly;
I set her down, wi' right good will,
  Amang the rigs o' barley:
I ken't her heart was a' my ain;
  I lov'd her most sincerely;
I kiss'd her owre and owre again,
  Amang the rigs o' barley.

I lock'd her in my fond embrace;
　Her heart was beating rarely:
My blessings on that happy place,
　Amang the rigs o' barley!
But by the moon and stars so bright,
　That shone that night so clearly!
She ay shall bless that happy night,
　Amang the rigs o' barley.

I hae been blythe wi' comrades dear;
　I hae been merry drinking;
I hae been joyfu' gath'rin' gear;
　I hae been happy thinking:
But a' the pleasures e'er I saw,
　Tho' three times doubl'd fairly,
That happy night was worth them a',
　Amang the rigs o' barley.

Robert Burns

2

Crabs: Tiree

We tied a worm of bacon fat
to a flat rock with string
and dropped it over the edge
into the clear water
of the bay. It fell gently

to the sand and the seaweed.
A tug told us we'd a bite
or we saw the crab itself
latch onto the ragged fat and pulled it
steadily out: this was the knack.

Too sudden, too sharp
and it dropped from its stone
shadow, so clumsily evading
its fate. But smoothly,
feeding the rough string

through fist upon fist
and they would come to us
like lumps of lava, water
sluicing from their backs.
Dumbly determined

they hung on
by one improbable claw
before the dull crack as they hit
the harbour wall, or the side
of the pails we kept them in.

Standing in a row,
four or five of us holiday kids
pulled out scores in a day, till each
bucket was a brackish mass
of fearsome crockery

bubbling below
its skin of salt water.
What happened to them all? —
our train of buckets, the great stench
of our summer sport.

It was a blond boy
from Glasgow finally pushed me in,
head over heels, from where
I crouched on the pier wall.
When I righted myself

I was waist deep in crab-
infested waters. No one
could pull me out. 'You must walk
to the shore,' my sister shouted
as I held my hands

high above my head,
thinking I could at least
save them. But how beautiful
it was all around me! The spatter
of green crofts

and deep blue lochans;
the cottontail; the buttercup
on the cropped foreshore. The sky
was depthless; all was silence.
And I was there

moving slowly through
this perfect blue wedge,
bearing terror in one hand, guilt
in the other, leaving the briefest wake
to mark my shame.

Tom Pow

3

from Of the Day Estival

The gloming comes, the day is spent,
The sun goes out of sight,
And painted is the Occident
With pourpour sanguine bright.

The skarlet nor the golden threid,
Who would their beawtie trie,
Are nathing like the colour reid
And beautie of the sky.

Our west horizon circuler,
Fra time the sunne be set,
Is all with rubies (as it wer)
Or rosis reid ou'rfret.

What pleasour were to waike and see,
Endlang a river cleare,
The perfite forme of everie tree
Within the deepe appeare!

The salmon out of cruifs and creils
Up hailed into skowts,
The bels and circles on the weills,
Throw lowpping of the trouts.

O then it were a seemely thing,
While all is still and calme,
The praise of God to play and sing,
With cornet and with shalme.

Bot now the birds with mony schout
Cals uther be their name:
'Ga, Billie, turne our gude about,
Now time is to go hame.'

With bellie fow the beastes belive
Are turned fra the come,
Quhilk soberly they hameward drive,
With pipe and lilting horne.

Throw all the land great is the gild
Of rustik folk that crie,
Of bleiting sheep fra they be fild,
Of calves and rowting ky.

All labourers drawes hame at even,
And can till uther say,
Thankes to the gracious God of heaven,
Quhilk send this summer day.

Alexander Hume

4

Unachievable hopes and unassuageable sorrows

Unachievable hopes and unassuageable sorrows
that lie like apples where they fall.

Maybe as some of the great religions say
we've been dropped behind the enemy lines,
Chindit, and lost our memory.

Peter McCarey

5

Follow the Rainfall

A downpour in the black gap of night, a sultry summer night

The rattle of rain on shed roofs, cats scamper for cover

A few fallen leaves sail away, bent like boats

Follow the rainfall – see where it leads

Gutter drain stream river estuary

Ocean cloud mountain

Burn loch

heart

John Rice

6

Faclan, eich-mhara

nam bhruadar bha mi nam ghrunnd na mara
agus thu fhèin nad chuan trom
a' leigeil do chudruim orm
agus d'fhaclan gaoil socair nam chluasan
an dràsda 's a-rithist
òrach grinn ainneamh
man eich-mhara, man notaichean-maise
sacsafonaichean beaga fleòdradh

Kevin MacNeil

Words, seahorses

i dreamt i was the seafloor and you were the weight
of ocean pressing down on me, your quiet words of
love in my ears now and again, golden, elegant and
strange, like seahorses, like grace-notes, tiny floating
saxophones

Kevin MacNeil

7

Driving at Night with My Dad

Open the window,
the cool summer night swooshes in.
My favourite music playing loud.

2 a.m. – summer's midnight –
neither of us can sleep
so we go for a night drive.

Stars crowd the sky
and twinkle at us in code.
Our headlights reply in light language.

A fox crosses, red and grey,
and arches under a fence:
rabbits run and a farm cat's eyes
catch our beam.
She stares at us for a second of stretched time . . .
. . . her eyes two new coins.

Through villages that are asleep,
past farms that are warm,
past houses that are dreaming,
under trees that are resting,
past birds that have no flight, no song.

I sense I am in some other country
where day, time, people no longer matter.
In this huge dark,
through the somewhere and the nowhere
of this uninhabited world,
I feel safe and secure
driving at night with my dad.

John Rice

8

The Lion an the Unicorn

The lion an the unicorn
Fechtin for the croon;
Up jumped the wee dog,
An knocked them baith doon.

Some gat white breid,
An some gat broon;
But the lion beat the unicorn,
Roon aboot the toun.

Anon.

9

So, we'll go no more a-roving

So, we'll go no more a-roving
   So late into the night,
Though the heart be still as loving,
   And the moon be still as bright.

For the sword outwears its sheath,
   And the soul wears out the breast,
And the heart must pause to breathe,
   And love itself have rest.

Though the night was made for loving,
   And the day returns too soon,
Yet we'll go no more a-roving
   By the light of the moon.

George Gordon, Lord Byron

10

Datur Hora Quieti

The sun upon the lake is low,
  The wild birds hush their song,
The hills have evening's deepest glow,
  Yet Leonard tarries long.
Now all whom varied toil and care
  From home and love divide,
In the calm sunset may repair
  Each to the loved one's side.

The noble dame on turret high,
  Who waits her gallant knight,
Looks to the western beam to spy
  The flash of armour bright.
The village maid, with hand on brow
  The level ray to shade,
Upon the footpath watches now
  For Colin's darkening plaid.

Now to their mates the wild swans row,
  By day they swam apart.
And to the thicket wanders slow
  The hind beside the hart.
The woodlark at his partner's side
  Twitters his closing song –
All meet whom day and care divide,
  But Leonard tarries long!

Sir Walter Scott

11

Verses written to the Queen of England

A single thought which benefits and harms me
Bitter and sweet alternate endlessly in my heart.
Between hope and fear this thought weighs down on me
So much that peace and rest flee from me.

So, dear sister, if this paper reiterates
My pressing desire to see you,
It is because I see in pain and sorrow
The immediate outcome if this request should fail.

I have seen the ship blown by contrary winds
On the high seas, near to the harbour mouth
And the calm turning to troubled water.

Likewise (sister) I live in fear and terror
Not on account of you, but because there are times
When Fortune can destroy sail and rigging at once.

Mary Queen of Scots

12

Five Mackerel

for Mary

Here's something
we can begin
to get our heads
around unlike

her summer
leaving

your kitchen
the unexpected
  mackerel

potato salad
with spring onion
big chunks
of apple

the hot, spitting fish
split easily
with the back
of the knife

Jen Hadfield

13

I'm sending you a letter

Inside, I put a full-size blue guitar, a slice of sea (so you could shake it in a glass over the Mediterranean coast), a saxophone I borrowed from a local busker because I know you'd like her work, all my air-miles, so you could come and visit me, a crow, crushed ice, a glass of pink champagne, just open carefully, mid-August Edinburgh (a bunch of slightly boozed-up actors, a box of unpredicted rain). I marked: fragile, FRAGILE, all over it. Let me know when it lands or crashes into your hands.

Stav Poleg

14

Gap Year

for Mateo

I.

I remember your Moses basket before you were born.
I'd stare at the fleecy white sheet for days, weeks,
willing you to arrive, hardly able to believe
I would ever have a real baby to put in the basket.

I'd feel the mound of my tight tub of a stomach,
and you moving there, foot against my heart,
elbow in my ribcage, turning, burping, awake, asleep.
One time I imagined I felt you laugh.

I'd play you Handel's Water Music or Emma Kirkby
singing Pergolesi. I'd talk to you, my close stranger,
call you Tumshie, ask when you were coming to meet me.
You arrived late, the very hot summer of eighty-eight.

You had passed the due date string of eights,
and were pulled out with forceps, blue, floury,
on the fourteenth of August on Sunday afternoon.
I took you home on Monday and lay you in your basket.

II.

Now, I peek in your room and stare at your bed
hardly able to imagine you back in there sleeping,
Your handsome face – soft, open. Now you are eighteen,
six foot two, away, away in Costa Rica, Peru, Bolivia.

I follow your trails on my Times Atlas:
from the Caribbean side of Costa Rica to the Pacific,
the baby turtles to the massive leatherbacks.
Then on to Lima, to Cuzco. Your grandfather

rings: 'Have you considered altitude sickness,
Christ, he's sixteen thousand feet above sea level.'
Then to the lost city of the Incas, Machu Picchu,
Where you take a photograph of yourself with the statue

of the original Tupac. You are wearing a Peruvian hat.
Yesterday in Puno before catching the bus for Copacabana,
you suddenly appear on a webcam and blow me a kiss,
you have a new haircut; your face is grainy, blurry.

Seeing you, shy, smiling, on the webcam reminds me
of the second scan at twenty weeks, how at that fuzzy
moment back then, you were lying cross-legged with
an index finger resting sophisticatedly on one cheek.

You started the Inca trail in Arctic conditions
and ended up in subtropical. Now you plan the Amazon
in Bolivia. Your grandfather rings again to say
'There's three warring factions in Bolivia, warn him

against it. He canny see everything. Tell him to come home.'
But you say all the travellers you meet rave about Bolivia.
You want to see the Salar de Uyuni,
the world's largest salt-flats, the Amazonian rainforest.

And now you are not coming home till four weeks after
your due date. After Bolivia, you plan to stay
with a friend's Auntie in Argentina.
Then – to Chile where you'll stay with friends of Diane's.

And maybe work for the Victor Jara Foundation.
I feel like a home-alone mother; all the lights
have gone out in the hall, and now I am
wearing your large black slippers, flip-flopping

into your empty bedroom, trying to imagine you
in your bed. I stare at the photos you send by messenger:
you on the top of the world, arms outstretched, eager.
Blue sky, white snow; you by Lake Tararhua, beaming.

My heart soars like the birds in your bright blue skies.
My love glows like the sunrise over the lost city.
I sing along to Ella Fitzgerald, A tisket A tasket.
I have a son out in the big wide world.

A flip and a skip ago, you were dreaming in your basket.

Jackie Kay

15

An Incomplete History of Rock Music in the Hebrides

Peewits quiffed like Elvis reel from rocks,
their sheen of feathers like blue suede
the breeze buffs in the midday air.
'He loves ewe. Meah! Meah! Meah!'
bleat a Fat Four of blackface sheep
beneath mop-tops of unshorn hair.

Jagged stalks of thistles strut,
flashing menace in the evening light
before a group of timeworn stones.
Spangled with glitter, starlings soar
and oystercatchers sport red lips
while herons stalk on platform soles.

Each fulmar packs its pistol.
There's anarchy on cliff-tops
as they reel and spit on rocks below.
Then a riff is played on marram grass,
shells syncopate on shorelines as
night downs its curtain on the show.

Donald S. Murray

16

The Temple of the Wood Lavender

A perfum'd sprig of lavender
You gave, dear child, to me;
It grew, you said, by the red rose bed,
And under the jessamine tree.

'Twas sweet, ay, sweet from many things;
But (sweeter than all) with scent
Of long past years and laughter and tears
It to me was redolent.

Lady Caroline Blanche Elizabeth Lindsay

17

Manly Sports

How brave is the hunter who nobly will dare
On horseback to follow the small timid hare;
Oh! ye soldiers who fall in defence of your flag,
What are you to the hero who brings down the stag?

Bright eyes glance admiring, soft hearts give their loves
To the knight who shoots best in 'the tourney of doves';
Nothing else with such slaughtering feats can compare,
To win manly applause, or the smiles of the fair.

A cheer for fox-hunting! Come all who can dare
Track this dangerous animal down to its lair;
'Tis first trapped, then set free for the huntsmen to follow
With horses and hounds, and with heartstirring halloo!

The brave knights on the moor when the grouse are a-drive,
Slay so many, you'd think, there'd be none left alive;
Oh! the desperate daring of slaughtering grouse,
Can only be matched in a real slaughterhouse.

The angler finds true Anglo-Saxon delight,
In trapping small fish, who so foolishly bite,
He enjoys the wild terror of creatures so weak,
And what manlier pleasures can anyone seek?

Marion Bernstein

18

Slate, Sea and Sky

An island on the rim of the world
in that space between slate, sea and sky
where air and ocean currents
are plays of wild energy
and the light changes everything.

Norman Bissell

19

A Birthday

I never felt so much
Since I have felt at all
The tingling smell and touch
Of dogrose and sweet briar,
Nettles against the wall,
All sours and sweets that grow
Together or apart
In hedge or marsh or ditch.
I gather to my heart
Beast, insect, flower, earth, water, fire,
In absolute desire,
As fifty years ago.

Acceptance, gratitude:
The first look and the last
When all between has passed
Restore ingenuous good
That seeks no personal end,
Nor strives to mar or mend.
Before I touched the food
Sweetness ensnared my tongue;
Before I saw the wood
I loved each nook and bend,
The track going right and wrong;
Before I took the road
Direction ravished my soul.
Now that I can discern

It whole or almost whole,
Acceptance and gratitude
Like travellers return
And stand where first they stood.

Edwin Muir

20

My Heart's in the Highlands

Farewell to the Highlands, farewell to the north,
The birth-place of Valour, the country of Worth;
Wherever I wander, wherever I rove,
The hills of the Highlands for ever I love.

Chorus
    My heart's in the Highlands, my heart is not here;
    My heart's in the Highlands, a-chasing the deer;
    A-chasing the wild-deer and following the roe,
    My heart's in the Highlands, wherever I go.

Farewell to the mountains high-cover'd with snow;
Farewell to the straths and green vallies below;
Farewell to the forests and wild-hanging woods;
Farewell to the torrents and loud-pouring floods.

Robert Burns

21

Be the first to like this

kicking pine cones down the street
climbing the backyard cherry tree
lying in new sheets
waking in darkness   waking to snow
how your chest thickens when you're scared
how your voice bubbles when you're pleased
be the first to like
view of wind turbines from the train
golden tint on a glass of wine
gliding on rollerblades by the sea
waking so warm   waking on the beach
how your eyes flood when you're tired
how you laugh when you're relieved
like bridges creeks Frisbees
silly cat videos and Instagram photos
like strolling with a friend
between folds of trees
and your heart rolls out a big pink wave
and your lips recall something sweet
like skiing and ice-skating
zip-lining above trees at seventy clicks
blood thudding in your ears
like every new experience because it was new
to you   pocketed in your memory
like the first time you fed the ducks
at Stanley Park
and they stormed like villagers
to your feet

Theresa Muñoz

22

The Bonny House o Airlie

It fell on a day, and a bonny simmer's day
When green grew aits and barley,
That there fell out a great dispute
Between Argyll and Airlie.

Argyll has raised a hunner men,
A hunner harnessed rarely,
And he's awa by the back o Dunkeld
To plunder the castle o Airlie.

Lady Ogilvie looks o'er her bower window,
And oh but she looks weary
When there she spies the great Argyll
Come to plunder the bonny house o Airlie.

'Come doon, come doon, my Lady Ogilvie,
Come doon and kiss me fairly.'
'O I winna kiss the fause Argyll
If he shouldna leave a standing stane in Airlie.'

He's taen her by the left shoulder,
Saying, 'Dame, where lies thy dowry?'
'O it's east and west o yon waterside
And it's doon by the banks o the Airlie.'

They hae sought it up, they hae sought it doon,
They hae sought it maist severely,
Till they fand it on the fair plum-tree
That shines on the bowling-green o Airlie.

He's taen her by the middle sae small,
And O, but she grat sairly!
And he's laid her down by the bonny burnside
Till they'd plundered the castle o Airlie.

'Gif my gude lord war here this nicht
As he is with King Chairlie,
Neither you nor ony ither Scottish lord
Durst avow to the plundering o Airlie.

'Gif my gude lord war now at hame,
As he is with his king,
There durst nae a Campbell in a' Argyll
Set fit on Airlie green.

'Ten bonny sons I have born unto him,
The eleventh ne'er saw his daddy;
But though I had a hunner mair
I'd gie them a' to King Chairlie.'

Anon.

23

A Lang Promise

Whether the weather be dreich or fair, my luve,
if guid times greet us, or we hae tae face the worst,
ahint and afore whit will happen tae us:
blind in the present, eyes open to the furore,
unkempt or perjink, suddenly puir or poorly,
peely-wally or in fine fettle, beld or frosty,
calm as a ghoul or in a feery-farry,
in dork December or in springy spring weather,
doon by the Barrows, on the Champs-Élysées,
at midnicht, first licht, whether the mune
be roond or crescent, and yer o' soond mind
or absent, I'll tak your trusty haun
and lead you over the haw – hame, ma darlin.
I'll carry ma lantern, and daur defend ye agin ony foe;
and whilst there is breath in me, I'll blaw it intae ye.
Fir ye are ma true luve, the bonnie face I see;
nichts I fall intae slumber, it's ye swimming up
in all yer guidness and blitheness, yer passion.
You'll be mine, noo, an' till the end o' time,
ma bonnie lassie, I'll tak the full guid o' ye'
and gie it back, and gie it back tae ye:
a furst kiss, a lang promise, time's gowden ring.

Jackie Kay

24

Mary's Song

I wad ha'e gi'en him my lips tae kiss,
Had I been his, had I been his;
Barley breid and elder wine,
Had I been his as he is mine.

The wanderin' bee it seeks the rose;
Tae the lochan's bosom the burnie goes;
The grey bird cries at evenin's fa',
'My luve, my fair one, come awa'.'

My beloved sall ha'e this he'rt tae break,
Reid, reid wine and the barley cake;
A he'rt tae break, an' a mou' tae kiss,
Tho' he be nae mine, as I am his.

Marion Angus

25

The Berries

When she came for me
through the ford, came for me
through running water
I was oxter-deep in a bramble-grove
glutting on wild fruit. Soon
we were climbing the same
sour gorge the river fled, fall
by noiseless fall. I mind
a wizened oak
cleaving the rock it grew from,
and once, a raptor's mewl.
Days passed – or what passed for days,
and just as I'd put the whole misadventure
down to something I ate,
she leapt twice, thrice, my sick
head spun, and here we were:
a vast glen ringed by snow-peaks,
sashaying grass, a scented breeze,
and winding its way toward us
that same world-river –
its lush banks grazed by horses, horses
I knew she'd leave me for,
right there, her own kin –
no use my pleas, no use
my stumbling back down
to where the berries grew,
because this is what I wanted,

so all I could do was brace myself
and loosen my grip from her mane.

Kathleen Jamie

26

from Farm by the Shore

small oats rye bere barley
ripe harvest in late summer
a shallow ploughing
grazing and fallow in rotation

corncrake and corn bunting
great yellow bumble bee
oystercatcher lapwing golden plover
orchid vetch and clover

when no one is home
the strawberry roan
stands in the rain
forlorn

mattress of heather
of bracken or eelgrass
pillow of cottongrass
stuffed with a down
of coltsfoot or reedmace
floor strewn with bog myrtle

strong rope of heather
honeysuckle bridle
twisted birch bark tether
fish trap of sedge
purple moor-grass anchor rope

Thomas A. Clark

27

Blaeberry Mou

The flitterin faces come doun the brae
And the baskets gowd and green;
And nane but a blindie wud speer the day
Whaur a' the bairns hae been.

The lift is blue, and the hills are blue,
And the lochan in atween;
But nane sae blue as the blaeberry mou'
That needna tell whaur it's been.

William Soutar

28

We'll Go to Sea No More

Oh! blythely shines the bonnie sun
 Upon the Isle of May,
And blythely comes the morning tide
 Into St Andrew's Bay;
Then up, gudeman – the breeze is fair;
 And up, my braw bairns three, –
There's goud in yonder bonnie boat
 That sails so well the sea!
  When haddocks leave the Firth of Forth,
   And mussels leave the shore;
  When oysters climb up Berwick Law,
   We'll go to sea no more,
     No more,
   We'll go to sea no more.

I've seen the waves as blue as air,
 I've seen them green as grass;
But I never feared their heaving yet,
 From Grangemouth to the Bass.
I've seen the sea as black as pitch,
 I've seen it white as snow;
But I never feared its foaming yet,
 Though the winds blew high or low.
  When squalls capsize our wooden walls,
   When the French ride at the Nore,
  When Leith meets Aberdour half-way,
   We'll go to sea no more,
     No more,
   We'll go to sea no more.

I never liked the landsman's life,
   The earth is aye the same;
Gi'e me the ocean for my dower,
   My vessel for my hame.
Gi'e me the fields that no man ploughs,
   The farm that pays no fee;
Gi'e me the bonny fish that glance
   So gladly through the sea.
      When sails hang flapping on the masts,
        While through the waves we snore;
      When in a calm we're tempest tost,
       We'll go to sea no more,
           No more,
      We'll go to sea no more.

The sun is up, and round Inchkeith
The breezes softly blaw;
The gudeman has his lines aboard, –
Awa', my bairns, awa'!
An' ye'll be back by gloaming gray,
An' bright the fire will low;
An' in our tales and sangs we'll tell
How weel the boat ye row. –
      When life's last sun gangs feebly down,
        And death comes to our door –
      When a' the warld's a dream, to us,
       We'll go to sea no more,
           No more,
      We'll go to sea no more.

Anon.

29

Bennachie

There's Tap o' Noth, the Buck, Ben Newe,
Lonach, Ben Rinnes, Lochnagar,
Mount Keen, an' mony a Carn I trow
That's smored in mist ayont Braemar.
Bauld Ben Macdhui towers until
Ben Nevis looms, the laird o' a';
But Bennachie! Faith, yon's the hill
Rugs at the hairt when ye're awa!

Schiehallion, – ay, I've heard the name –
Ben More, the Ochils, Arthur's Seat,
Tak them an a' your hills o' fame
Wi' lochans leamin' at their feet;
But set me doon by Gadie side,
Or whaur the Glenton lies by Don –
The muircock an' the whaup for guide
Up Bennachie I'm rivin' on.

Syne on the Mither Tap sae far
Win'-cairdit clouds drift by abeen,
An' wast ower Keig stands Callievar
Wi' a' the warld to me, atween.
There's braver mountains ower the sea,
An' fairer haughs I've kent, but still
The Vale o' Alford! Bennachie!
Yon is the howe, an' this the hill!

Charles Murray

30

Memorial

Everywhere she dies. Everywhere I go she dies.
No sunrise, no city square, no lurking beautiful
    mountain
but has her death in it.
The silence of her dying sounds through
the carousel of language, it's a web
on which laughter stitches itself. How can my hand
clasp another's when between them
is that thick death, that intolerable distance?

She grieves for my grief. Dying, she tells me
that bird dives from the sun, that fish
leaps into it. No crocus is carved more gently
than the way her dying
shapes my mind. – But I hear, too,
the other words,
black words that make the sound
of soundlessness, that name the nowhere
she is continuously going into.

Ever since she died
she can't stop dying. She makes me her elegy.
I am a walking masterpiece,
a true fiction
of the ugliness of death.
I am her sad music.

Norman MacCaig

31

Lost Loch Floating

Lost loch floating
behind the mist
summer
is over.

Kevin MacNeil

September

I

The Sorting Hat Song

Oh you may not think I'm pretty,
But don't judge on what you see,
I'll eat myself if you can find
A smarter hat than me.
You can keep your bowlers black,
Your top hats sleek and tall,
For I'm the Hogwarts Sorting Hat
And I can cap them all.
There's nothing hidden in your head
The Sorting Hat can't see,
So try me on and I will tell you
Where you ought to be.
You might belong in Gryffindor,
Where dwell the brave at heart,
Their daring, nerve, and chivalry
Set Gryffindors apart;
You might belong in Hufflepuff,
Where they are just and loyal,
Those patient Hufflepuffs are true
And unafraid of toil;
Or yet in wise old Ravenclaw,
If you've a ready mind,
Where those of wit and learning,
Will always find their kind;
Or perhaps in Slytherin
You'll make your real friends,
Those cunning folks use any means

To achieve their ends.
So put me on! Don't be afraid!
And don't get in a flap!
You're in safe hands (though I have none)
For I'm a Thinking Cap!

J. K. Rowling

The Ponies

Here they come, trotting
 toward the bearers of kind words.

Beyond their field, the westernmost,
a rampart rises of cobble-stones and sea-weed,
then an ocean they'll never behold.

Tear down the fences!
Set the ponies free!

 Till then, though
we name them for the fishing boats
tied up in the harbour:
 the *Welcome Home*, the *Merlin*
  – and this tough wee Sheltie
chewing, look! your sketch-book –
   she is the *Radiant Queen.*

Kathleen Jamie

3

Three Lyrics

Love invents the year, the day
the hour and its melody;
love invents the lover, even
the beloved. Nothing is proven
against love that the mouth you kissed
so hungrily did not exist.

Lines for two sides of a fan:
– I desire you to forget –
– I forget you to desire –

I'd paint you, alone
on the latter-day urn
of an old photograph,
or the mirror's false depths –
alive to your heart,
dead to your poet

Don Paterson

4

Hiding Places

The world beneath the table
When no one knows you're there,
The second home that's all your own
Underneath the stair.

Your bedroom when you shut the door
And in the mirror see
This quite fantastic person who
You know you're going to be.

The space above the wardrobe where
Your best-kept secrets nest,
The attic that's a hideout when
Your parent is a pest.

The hideaway inside your head
Contains a magic light,
Just switch it on and you can zap
All monsters of the night.

A person needs a hiding place –
Four walls alone won't do.
You need a corner, secret, quiet,
to grow you into you.

Diana Hendry

5

Island School

A boy leaves a small house
   Of sea light. He leaves
   The sea smells, creel
   And limpet and cod.

The boy walks between steep
   Stone houses, echoing
   Gull cries, the all-around
   Choirs of the sea,

Ship noises, shop noises, clamours
   of bellman and milkcart.
   The boy comes at last
   To a tower with a tall desk

And a globe and a blackboard
   And a stem chalk-
   smelling lady. A bell
   Nods and summons.

A girl comes, cornlight
   In the eyes, smelling
   Of peat and cows
   And the rich midden.

Running she comes, late,
  Reeling in under the last
  Bronze brimmings. She sits
Among twenty whispers.

George Mackay Brown

6

Who's Who

When it arrives for processing
on my library office desk I flip through *Who's Who*

as self-consciously as if
I were scanning the Personal Columns.

Your list of achievements
are too familiar to impress
but it's an unlooked for thrill
to read your unexpected middle name.

One morning
I datestamp with more vigour than usual
a magazine with your face on the cover.

I almost drop a cup
when you ease yourself over the airwaves
into my kitchen;

spinning round to stare
blushing at the radio

I smooth my apron,
tuck back a loose strand
of greasy hair.

Angela McSeveney

'Poussie, poussie, baudrons'

'Poussie, poussie, baudrons,
Whaur hae ye been?'
'I've been tae London,
Tae see the queen!'

'Poussie, poussie, baudrons,
Whit gat ye there?'
'I gat a guid fat mousikie,
Rinnin up a stair!'

'Poussie, poussie, baudrons,
Whit did ye dae wi it?'
'I pit it in ma meal-poke,
Tae eat it wi' ma breid!'

Anon.

8

The Fairy School under the Loch

The wind sings its gusty song.
The bell rings its rusty ring.
The underwater fairy children
dive and swim through school gates.
They do not get wet.

The waves flick their flashing spray.
A school of fish wriggles its scaly way.
The underwater fairy children
learn their liquidy lessons.
Their reading books are always dry.

The seals straighten in a stretchy mass.
Teresa the Teacher flits and floats from class to class.
The underwater fairy children
count, play, sing and recite,
their clothes not in the least bit damp.

The rocks creak in their cracking skin.
A fairy boat drifts into a loch of time.
The underwater fairy children
lived, learned and left this life –
their salty stories now dry as their cracked wings.

John Rice

9

Lament for Flodden

I've heard them lilting at our ewe-milking,
  Lasses a' lilting before dawn o' day;
But now they are moaning on ilka green loaning –
  The Flowers of the Forest are a' wede away.

At bughts, in the morning, nae blythe lads are scorning,
  Lasses are lonely and dowie and wae;
Nae daffin', nae gabbin', but sighing and sabbing,
  Ilk ane lifts her leglin and hies her away.

In har'st, at the shearing, nae youths now are jeering,
  Bandsters are lyart, and runkled, and grey;
At fair or at preaching, nae wooing, nae fleeching –
  The Flowers of the Forest are a' wede away.

At e'en, in the gloaming, nae younkers are roaming
  'Bout stacks wi' the lasses at bogle to play;
But ilk ane sits drearie, lamenting her dearie –
  The Flowers of the Forest are weded away.

Dool and wae for the order, sent our lads to the Border!
  The English, for ance, by guile wan the day;
The Flowers of the Forest, that fought ay the foremost,
  The prime of our land, are cauld in the clay.

We'll hear nae mair lilting at the ewe-milking;
　Women and bairns are heartless and wae;
Sighing and moaning on ilka green loaning –
　The Flowers of the Forest are a' wede away.

Jean Elliot

10

Ossian's Grave

In the Highlands of Scotland I love,
Storm clouds curve down on the dark fields and strands,
With icy grey mist closing in from above –
Here Ossian's grave still stands.
In dreams my heart races to be there,
To deeply breathe in its native air –
And from this long-forgotten shrine
Take its second life as mine.

Alan Riach

11

from The Gruffalo (Scots)

A moose took a dauner through the deep, mirk widd.
A tod saw the moose and the moose looked guid.
'Whaur are ye aff tae, wee broon moose?
Will ye no hae yer denner in ma deep-doon hoose?'
'That's awfie kind o ye, Tod, but I'll no –
I'm gonnae hae ma denner wi a gruffalo.'
'A gruffalo? Whit's a gruffalo then?'
'A gruffalo! Whit, dae ye no ken?
He has muckle lang tusks,
and muckle big paws,
And muckle sherp teeth in his muckle strang jaws.'
'Whaur are ye meetin him?'
'By these stanes, the noo.
And his favourite food is hot tod stew.'
'Hot tod stew! I'm no here!' Tod yelped.
'See ye efter, wee moose,' and awa he skelped.
'See yon Tod! Is he daft or no?
There's nae such thing as a gruffalo!'

Julia Donaldson

12

Life-cycle of the Moth

Each word or phrase is the name of an actual moth.

Peach-blossom, muslin. Sallow kitten,
Gipsy.

Dark tussock, satin carpet.
Wood-leopard, scarlet tiger!

Great prominent,
Iron prominent –
Dark crimson underwing.

Emperor, white ermine,
Large emerald.

December. Frosted green.
Lackey, red-necked footman.
Drinker.
Scarce silver.

Old lady,
Figure of eighty,
Death's head,
Vapourer.

Ghost swift.

Elma Mitchell

13

The Airmen

Have you heard those birds of the morning
    That rise with the lark's first flight?
Have you seen those birds of shadow
    That pounce with the owl at night?
They swoop where hell is flaming,
    They soar in heaven apart.
They fly with the swallow's swiftness,
    And fight with the eagle's heart.

Have you seen their glinting feathers?
    They are off to the Fields of Fate,
Where the flowers all wear scarlet,
    And the rivers red are in spate.
To prick new names of glory
    On valour's ancient chart,
They fly with the swallow's swiftness
    And fight with the eagle's heart.

Have you heard their thrumming music?
    It drones to the cannon's boom
And the wailing whizz of the shrapnel
    Like an undersong of doom.
Wherever in loudest chorus
    The deafening thunders start,
They fly with the swallow's swiftness,
    And fight with the eagle's heart.

And though some of the first and fleetest
  Have flown away to the west,
And sunk on the seas of twilight
  With a wound in their shining breast,
The others know that, homing,
  In the end all birds depart,
And they fly with the swallow's swiftness,
  And fight with the eagle's heart.

Have you seen those birds of the morning
  That rout the carrion crow?
Have you seen those birds of shadow
  That pounce on the stoat below?
Till Hell recalls its legions,
  And Death lays down his dart,
They'll fly with the swallow's swiftness,
  And fight with the eagle's heart.

Margaret Armour

14

Autumn Fires

In the other gardens
  And all up the vale,
From the autumn bonfires
  See the smoke trail!

Pleasant summer over
  And all the summer flowers,
The red fire blazes,
  The grey smoke towers.

Sing a song of seasons!
  Something bright in all!
Flowers in the summer,
  Fires in the fall!

Robert Louis Stevenson

15

Be-Ro

The pages have browned like the gingerbread,
the rock cakes, treacle scones and Victoria sponges
she used to bake for us.

The pancake recipes are almost illegible,
stuck together years ago
by drops of ancient batter.

Not that she would have needed a recipe,
after the dozens she had flipped
on old kitchen ranges, girdles and stoves.

Just above the Madeira Cake
the small hand of one of her daughters
has pencilled in: This BoOk BeLongs to MUMMY.

Next to the Cherry Cake and Melting Moments
her own handwriting runs down the page
multiplying the ingredients by three or four.

I don't remember ever thanking her,
as the still warm baking disappeared
like snow off a dyke.

Angela McSeveney

16

I have a little nut-tree

I have a little nut-tree
Nothing will it bear
But a silver anguish
And a golden tear.

Now in return for the kiss
You gave to me
I hand you the fruit of
My little nut-tree.

Veronica Forrest-Thomson

17

A Country Boy Goes to School

I.
There he is, first lark this year
   Loud, between
That raincloud and the sun, lost
Up there, a long sky run, what peltings of song!
   (Six times 6, 36. Six times 7, 42
   Six times eight is . . .)
Oh, Mr Ferguson, have mercy at arithmetic time
   On peedie Tom o' the Glebe.

II.
There's Gyre's ewe has 2 lambs.
   Snow on the ridge still.
How many more days do I have to take
This peat under my oxter
   For the school fire?
   (James the Sixth, Charles the First . . . Who then?)
Oh, Mr Ferguson, I swear
   I knew all the Stewarts last night.

III.
Yes, Mistress Wylie, we're all fine.
   A pandrop! Oh, thank you.
I must hurry, Mistress Wylie,
   Old Ferguson
Gets right mad if a boy's late.
I was late twice last week.
   Do you know this, Mistress Wylie,

The capital of Finland is Helsingfors . . .
Yes, I'll tell Grannie
 You have four fat feese this summer.

IV.
When I get to the top of the brae
I'll see the kirk, the school, the shop,
 Smithy and inn and boatyard.
I wish I was that tinker boy
Going on over the hill, the wind in his rags.

Look, the schoolyard's like a throng of bees.

V.
I wish Willie Thomson
 Would take me on his creel-boat!
'Tom, there's been six generations of Corstons
 Working the Glebe,
And I doubt there'll never be fish-scales
On your hands, or salt in your boots . . .'

(Sixteen ounces, one pound. Fourteen pounds, one stone.)
A sack of corn's a hundredweight.
 I think a whale must be bigger than a ton.

VI.
Jimmo Spence, he told me
 Where the lark's nest is.
 Besides a stone in his father's oatfield,
 The high granite corner.

('I wandered lonely as a cloud . . .' Oh where? What then?)
I could go up by the sheep track
   Now the scholars are in their pen
And *Scallop* and *Mayflower* are taking the flood
   And the woman of Fea
Is pinning her washing to the wind.

I could wait for the flutter of the lark coming down.

VII.
The school bell! Oh, my heart's
Pounding louder than any bell.

   A quarter of a mile to run.
   My bare feet
   Have broken three daffodils in the field.

Heart thunderings, last tremor of the bell
   And the lark wing-folded.

'Late again, Master Thomas Corston of the Glebe farm.
Enter, sir. With the greatest interest
   We all await your explanation
Of a third morning's dereliction.'

George Mackay Brown

18

There was a Sang

There was a sang
That aye I wad be singin',
There was a star,
An' clear it used tae shine;
An' liltin' in the starlicht
Thro' the shadows
I gaed lang syne.

There was a sang;
But noo, I canna mind it.
There was a star,
But noo, it disna shine.
There was a luve that led me
Thro' the shadows –
And it *was* mine.

Helen B. Cruickshank

19

The Loch Ness Monster

Sometimes at night when the wind blows hard
the Loch Ness monster is lonely
for his extinct contemporaries
the warm flying fox and the luscious algae

so too in the long silent hours when the wind blows
(the black water closing over my head)
I am lonely for you my extinct love
pinioned down there in the strata

'I love you' I cry –
but you cannot weep or move your head

and I am terrified I shall not be near you again
until the rocks are broken
and our dead dust is blown out into space.

Tom Buchan

20

Lachlan Gorach's Rhyme

First the heel,
An than the toe,
That's the wey
The polka goes.

First the toe,
An than the heel,
That's the wey
Tae dance a reel.

Quick aboot,
An than away,
Lichtlie dance
The gled Strathspey.

Jump a jump
An jump it big,
That's the wey
Tae dance a jig,

Slowly, smiling,
As in France,
Follow through
The country dance.

And we'll meet Johnnie Cope in the mornin.

Anon.

21

Johnnie Cope

Cope sent a challenge frae Dunbar:
'Charlie, meet me an' ye daur,
An' I'll learn you the art o' war
If you'll meet me i' the morning.'

Chorus
    Hey, Johnnie Cope, are ye wauking yet?
    Or are your drums a-beating yet?
    If ye were wauking I wad wait
    To gang to the coals i' the morning.

When Charlie looked the letter upon
He drew his sword the scabbard from:
'Come, follow me, my merry merry men,
And we'll meet Johnnie Cope i' the morning.'

Chorus

'Now Johnnie, be as good's your word;
Come, let us try both fire and sword;
And dinna rin like a frichted bird,
That's chased frae its nest i' the morning.'

Chorus

When Johnnie Cope he heard of this,
He thought it wadna be amiss
To hae a horse in readiness,
To flee awa' i' the morning.

Chorus

Fy now, Johnnie, get up an' rin;
The Highland bagpipes mak' a din;
It's best to sleep in a hale skin,
For 'twill be a bluidy morning.

Chorus

When Johnnie Cope tae Dunbar came,
They speired at him, 'Where's a' your men?'
'The deil confound me gin I ken,
For I left them a' i' the morning.

Chorus

'Now Johnnie, troth, ye werena blate
To come wi' news o' your ain defeat,
And leave your men in sic a strait
Sae early in the morning.

Chorus

'I' faith,' quo' Johnnie, 'I got sic flegs
Wi' their claymores an' philabegs;
If I face them again, deil break my legs!
Sae I wish you a' gude morning.'

Anon.

22

Grey Geese

All night they flew over in skeins.
I heard their wrangling far away
Went out once to look for them, long
    after midnight.
Saw them silvered by the moonlight, like waves,
Flagging south, jagged and tired,
Across the sleeping farms and the autumn rivers
To the late fields of autumn.

Even in a city I have heard them
Their noise like the rusty wheel of a bicycle;
I have looked up from among the drum of engines
To find them in the sky
A broken arrowhead turning south
Heading for home.

The Iceland summer, the long light
Has run like rivers through their wings,
Strengthened the sinews of their flight
Over the whole ocean, till at last they circle,
Straggle down on the chosen runway of
    their field.

They come back
To the same place, the same day, without fail;
Precision instruments, a compass
Somewhere deep in their souls.

Kenneth C. Steven

The Teachers

they taught
that what you wrote in ink
carried more weight than what you wrote in pencil
and could not be rubbed out.
Punctuation was difficult. Wars
were bad but sometimes necessary
in the face of absolute evil as they knew only too well.
Miss Prentice wore her poppy the whole month of
    November.
Miss Mathieson hit the loud pedal
on the piano and made us sing
The Flowers of the Forest.
Miss Ferguson deplored the Chinese custom
of footbinding but extolled the ingenuity
of terracing the paddyfields.
Someone she'd once known
had given her a kimono and a parasol.

Miss Prentice said the Empire had enlightened people
and been a two-way thing.
The Dutch grew bulbs and were our allies in
wooden shoes.

We grew bulbs on the window sills
beside the frogspawn that quickened into wriggling
commas or stayed full stop.
Some people in our class were stupid, full stop.
The leather tawse was coiled around the sweetie tin
in her desk beside the box of coloured blackboard chalk
Miss Ferguson never used.

Miss Prentice wore utility smocks.
Miss Mathieson had a moustache.
If your four-needled knitting got no
further than the heel you couldn't turn
then she'd keep you at your helio sewing
till its wobbling cross-stitch was specked with rusty blood.

Spelling hard words was easy when you knew how.

Liz Lochhead

24

Jock since ever I saw your face

Jock since ever I saw yer face
  Jock since ever I kent ye
Jock since ever I saw yer face
  dae ye mind o' the shillin' I lent ye?

Lost ma love an' I dinna ken hoo
  lost ma love an' I care na'
the losin' o' wan's the gainin' o' twa
  I'll find me another I fear na'.

Anon.

25

The Stars of Autumn

We stood below the stars of autumn, and
Whispering with me you proved you knew
That they, also, die. I touched your hand.
We stood below the stars of autumn. And,
Shivering, I tried to say what I had planned,
But did not (though it all came true).
We stood below the stars of autumn, and
Whispering with me, you proved you knew.

Gerry Cambridge

26

People Etcetera

People are lovely to touch –
A nice warm sloppy tilting belly
Happy in its hollow of pelvis
Like a bowl of porridge.

People are fun to notice –
Their eyes taking off like birds
Away from their words
To settle on breasts and ankles
Irreverent as pigeons.

People are good to smell –
Leathery, heathery, culinary or Chanel,
Lamb's-wool, sea-salt, linen dried in the wind,
Skin fresh out of a shower.

People are delicious to taste –
Crisp and soft and tepid as new-made bread,
Tangy as blackberries, luscious as avocado,
Native as milk,
Acrid as truth.

People are irresistible to draw —
Hand following hand,
Eye outstaring eye,
Every curve an experience of self,
Felt weight of flesh, tension of muscle
And all the geology of an elderly face.

And people are easy to write about?
Don't say it.
What are these shadows
Vanishing
Round the
Corner?

Elma Mitchell

27

Requiem

Under the wide and starry sky,
Dig the grave and let me lie.
Glad did I live and gladly die,
  And I laid me down with a will.

This be the verse you grave for me:
Here he lies where he longed to be;
Home is the sailor, home from sea,
  And the hunter home from the hill.

Robert Louis Stevenson

28

Crab-Apples

My mother picked crab-apples
off the Glasgow apple trees
and pounded them with chillies
to change
her homesickness
into green chutney.

Imtiaz Dharker

29

The Cat's Tale

The cat doesn't understand
about reading
or the space between
my eyes and the paper
or the stillness.
The silence.

She pops up
between my propped elbows
soft as peach and ashes
under my chin
executes feline twirls
then lodges her tail
below my nose
so I can smell
how clean she is.

She sits on the page
translates the words
into thrumming
cheek-butts my nose
jaggy-licks my eyelid shut
and spins me
a compelling tale
of love beyond words.

Valerie Thornton

30

The Royal High School

After the children had gone
the gulls came, in a white flit:
sentinel at windows,
falling between buildings.
The janitors and cleaners never saw them
dropping in: ambling down corridors,
looking into rooms, blinking
at their new estate.
They nest here now, among the jotters
and pencils, unopened boxes
of *The Scottish Constitution*;
living like kings
on a diet of silverfish,
long-life milk and chalk.

Robin Robertson

October

I

Shores

If we were in Talisker on the shore
where the great white foaming mouth of water
opens between two jaws as hard as flint –
the Headland of Stones and the Red Point –
I'd stand forever by the waves
renewing love out of their crumpling graves
as long as the sea would be going over
the Bay of Talisker forever;
I would stand there by the filling tide
till Preshal bowed his stallion head.

And if the two of us were together
on the shores of Calgary in Mull
between Scotland and Tiree,
between this world and eternity,
I'd stand there till time was done
counting the sands grain by grain.
And also on Uist, on Hosta's shore,
in the face of solitude's fierce stare,
I'd remain standing, without sleep,
while sea were ebbing, drop by drop.

And if I were on Moidart's shore
with you, my novelty of desire,
I'd offer this synthesis of love,
grain and water, sand and wave.
And were we by the shelves of Staffin
where the huge joyless sea is coughing
stones and boulders from its throat,
I'd build a fortified wall
against eternity's savage howl.

Sorley MacLean,
translated by Iain Crichton Smith

2

Reading by a Window

My finger catches the edge of a page,
and through the glass half-grown boys
play shinty, calling like crows, spinning
the ball across the grass. The paper
flutters the peaceful print. I am greedy
for words, cram and taste them, loose
them, reckless, into the bloodstream. A boy
pivots on his heel, an arm wide
as a wing. The water behind his head
blends cloud and supple islands.

Gulls balance above the boys'
swooping awkwardness. History
wheels. With my book open in my hands
the glass reveals a rehearsal of the past,
of boys shouting and turning, a boat
braced on the loch. For boys have run
on this shore since stories began, and wind
has driven the sails of the herring hunters.

The page settles, now cradling the tranquil
print. But the words are restive, shake
the window, call like boys or crows.
Spindles of smoke roll on the shore,
blurring the fire and the salt-bleached wood.
Under a diffident sun the boys
throw their bodies on the ground. The page
traps their breaking voices, suddenly
holds them hostage for the coming story.

Jenni Daiches

3

The Memory of Timber

by want –
as in 'I want you' and

'I want to write' – I mean
as if the sap in the floorboards candled

and began to flow – bruises freshening
round the cleats and congealed grain

loosening like lava around the nails and knots
to giddy in lees where flour-gold would gather

were floorboards a river

I want –

no wonder the cat skips and shivers
and stares up wildly

into empty corners –

the knots scorch the shirred flesh
in their readiness

to spout scaled limbs –
the knots are the shape of sparrows'

breasts puffed up against
a snow-strafed wind

Jen Hadfield

4

O, Wert Thou in the Cauld Blast

O, wert thou in the cauld blast
   On yonder lea, on yonder lea,
My plaidie to the angry airt,
   I'd shelter thee, I'd shelter thee.
Or did Misfortune's bitter storms
   Around thee blaw, around thee blaw,
Thy bield should be my bosom,
   To share it a', to share it a'.

Or were I in the wildest waste,
   Sae black and bare, sae black and bare,
The desert were a Paradise,
   If thou wert there, if thou wert there.
Or were I monarch o the globe,
   Wi thee to reign, wi thee to reign,
The brightest jewel in my crown
   Wad be my queen, wad be my queen.

Robert Burns

5

Skye nocturne

We lie on hard ground
under a map of stars
sensing the inky outline of high hills.

Beyond the midnight breeze
a lonely curlew pipes her eerie note
while nearer by the tent flaps lazily.

I turn to you
and pull your sleeping body close,
curling myself about you.

The form, the heft, the warmth
of you, are all I know
or need to know.

Say nothing to me now
for I am overcome
by this touching proximity.

Or say what impulse you have jogged
in the dry white boneyard of my heart
in this Glen Brittle.

Gordon Jarvie

6

Saw ye Eppie Marly, honey?

Saw ye Eppie Marly, honey,
The wife that sells the barley, honey?
She's lost her pocket an a' her money,
Wi followin Jacobite Charlie, honey.

Eppie Marly's turned sae fine,
She'll no gang oot tae herd the swine,
But lies in bed till echt or nine,
An winna come doon the stairs tae dine.

Anon.

7

Leaving Stromness

always, the salt, the tear:

nestled houses gather distance
solid on the hill, unblinking

till, on the Ness, one handkerchief,
one arm waving

Anne MacLeod

8

An acarsaid

na rionnagan a' deàrrsadh 'san uisge
na rionnagan a' deàrrsadh na mo chridhe
an Cuan Sgìth mar sgàthan dorch
's do phòg mu dheireadh
air mo ghruaidh fhathast
balbh, fuar, fad air falbh
mar seann ghealach
a' cuimhneachadh air acarsaid eile

Kevin MacNeil

The harbour

the stars shining in the water the stars shining in
my heart the Minch like a dark mirror and your
farewell kiss still on my cheek – dumb, cold, distant
– like an old moon remembering another harbour

Kevin MacNeil

9

Wee Willie Winkie

Wee Willie Winkie
Rins through the toun,
Up stairs and doon stairs
In his nicht-goun,
Tirlin at the winnock,
Cryin at the lock,
'Are the weans in their bed?
For it's noo ten o'clock.'

Hey, Willie Winkie,
Are ye comin ben?
The cat's singin grey thrums
Tae the sleepin hen,
The dog's speldered on the flair,
An disna gie a cheep,
But here's a waukrife laddie
That winna fa asleep.

Onything but sleep, ye rogue!
Glowerin like the mune,
Rattlin in an airn jug
Wi an airn spune,
Rumbling, tumblin, roond aboot,
Crawin like a cock,
Skirlin like a kenna-whit,
Wauknin sleepin folk.

Hey, Willie Winkie –
The wean's in a creel!
Wamblin aff a body's knee
Like a verra eel,
Ruggin at the cat's lug,
Ravelin a' her thrums –
Hey, Willie Winkie –
See, there he comes!

William Miller

10

The Wild Geese

'Oh, tell me what was on yer road, ye roarin' norlan' wind,
As ye cam' blawin' frae the land that's niver frae my mind?
My feet they trayvel England, but I'm deein' for the north –'
'My man, I heard the siller tides rin up the Firth o' Forth.'

'Aye, Wind, I ken them well eneuch, and fine they fa' and
    rise,
And fain I'd feel the creepin' mist on yonder shore that lies,
But tell me, ere ye passed them by, what saw ye on the way?'
'My man, I rocked the rovin' gulls that sail abune the Tay.'

'But saw ye naethin', leein' Wind, afore ye cam to Fife?
There's muckle lyin' yont the Tay that's mair to me nor life.'
'My man, I swept the Angus braes ye haena trod for years –'
'O wind, forgie a hameless loon that canna see for tears!'

'And far abune the Angus straths I saw the wild geese flee,
A lang, lang skein o' beatin' wings wi' their heids towards the sea,
And aye their cryin' voices trailed abint them on the air –'
'O Wind, hae maircy, haud yer whisht, for I daurna listen
    mair!'

Violet Jacob

11

Rannoch Loop

Back here, the iron line crosses future, past:
Then my father will surely be seen

Trekking the sodden, lonely land,
Weekenders, together –

Or trudging through the ancient pine woods,
The musk smell of red deer,

My father, here on the moor,
Years and years after he's gone,

Held by the land's callused hands.
Och – big hikes across time, lochs, bogs,

September weekend or Easter, far flung,
Doon by Loch Ericht, on the west side

To the old crofter's burnt-out croft,
Still a magnificent doss, and he'll doss there,

(Twelve men to the wee hoose)
And rest, rest, till finally refreshed.

Rannoch Moor, Rannoch dear.
Beloved best, the best: back here.

Jackie Kay

12

Shandwick Stone

As jets without the black box of memory
startle sheep in deserted glens
the stone hunters stalk their various prey.

Chaotic and recurrent as the tides
incised patterns swirl underneath them.
The Pictish beast, that composite

bird-fish-mammal, harbours a smile
having already weathered eras and elements
untraceable by radar.

The rain-clouds gather above an unyielding sea.
Wildflowers and seeding grasses rustle
in anticipation of the next downpour.

Ken Cockburn

13

Scotland

Here in the uplands
The soil is ungrateful
The fields, red with sorrel,
Are stony and bare.
A few trees, wind-twisted –
Or are they but bushes?
Stand stubbornly guarding
A home here and there.

Scooped out like a saucer,
The land lies before me;
The waters, once scattered,
Flow orderly now
Through fields where the ghosts
Of the marsh and the moorland
Still ride the old marches,
Despising the plough.

The marsh and the moorland
Are not to be banished;
The bracken and the heather,
The glory of broom,
Usurp all the balks
And the field's broken fringes,
And claim from the sower
Their portion of room.

This is my country,
The land that begat me,
These windy spaces
Are surely my own.
And those who here toil
In the sweat of their faces
Are flesh of my flesh,
And bone of my bone.

Hard is the day's task
Scotland, stern Mother –
Wherewith at all times
Thy sons have been faced:
Labour by day,
And scant rest in the gloaming
With Want an attendant,
Not lightly outpaced.

Yet do thy children
Honour and love thee.
Harsh is thy schooling,
Yet great is the gain:
True hearts and strong limbs,
The beauty of faces,
Kissed by the wind
And caressed by the rain.

Sir Alexander Gray

14

The Bridge Over the Border

Here, I should surely think of home –
my country and the neat steep town
where I grew up: its banks of cloud,
the winds and changing, stagey light,
its bouts of surly, freezing rain, or failing that,

the time the train stuck here half an hour.
It was hot, for once. The engine seemed
to grunt and breathe with us,
and in the hush, the busker at the back
plucked out *Scotland the Brave*. There was

a filmic, golden light and the man opposite
was struck, he said, with love.
He saw a country in my eyes.
But he was from Los Angeles,
and I was thinking of another bridge.

It was October. I was running to meet a man
with whom things were not quite settled,
were not, in fact, to ever settle, and I stopped
halfway to gaze at birds – swallows
in their distant thousands, drawn

to Africa, or heat, or home, not knowing
which, but certain how. Shifting on the paper sky,
they were crosses on stock-market graphs,
they were sand in a hoop shaken sideways,
and I stared, as if panning for gold.

Kate Clanchy

15

Climbing the World

Heading home, the faces
of the passengers opposite
are reflected dark blue
in the late-night train windows.

I doze, my daughter yawns.

The head of the sleeping man
next to me lolls about like a puppet's.
His paperback slips from his lap
and falls on to the orange peel
he discarded before falling asleep.

He wakes in time to get off at Sevenoaks.

I pick up the book, brush the peel off the jacket.
It's *The Diary of a Young Girl: Anne Frank*,
the '97 Penguin edition, due back
at Paddington Library by 13 Dec.
I start reading the foreword

. . . Anne Frank kept a diary . . .

Her father, Otto Frank, edited her diaries
after she was dead.
I see him crying at the typewriter.

My daughter is twenty-seven.
We have great times together.
She is my friend and I love her.
Even in a train's harsh light she is very beautiful.
She is climbing the world.

Anne and Otto Frank
have taught me how to tell you this.

I shall now return the sleeping man's
book to Paddington Library.

John Rice

16

Love Shall Stay

The rose is dead, and the honey-bee
Forsakes the empty flower,
And summer has sailed across the sea,
Away from a leafless bower.

And the singing birds, to the siren south,
Have followed the sunbeam's track,
And never a word in his frozen mouth
Has the year to hail them back.

And rosy Love, with his eyes of dawn,
And his cheek of dimpling laughter –
How shall he live where the skies are wan?
Ah me! Will he up, and after?

The swallow may go, and the sun depart,
And the rose's bloom decay,
But I'll make a summer within my heart,
And Love, sweet Love, shall stay!

Margaret Armour

17

Crystal Set

Just as the stars appear, father
carries from his garden shed
a crystal set, built
as per instructions
in the *Amateur Mechanic*.
Mother dries her hands. Their boy
and ginger cat lie beside the fire.
He's reading – what –*Treasure Island* –
but jumps to clear the dresser. Hush,
they tell each other. Hush!

The silly baby bangs her spoon
as they lean in to radio-waves
which lap, the boy imagines,
just like Scarborough. Indeed,
it *is* the sea they hear as though
the brown box were a shell. Dad
sorts through fizz, until, like diamonds
lost in the dust – '*Listen, Ships' Morse!*'–
and the boy grips his chair. As though
he'd risen sudden as an angel
to gaze down, he understands
that not his house, not
Scarborough Beach, but the whole
Island of Britain
is washed by dark waves. Hush
they tell each other. Hush.

There is nothing to tune to
but Greenwich pips
and the anxious signalling
of ships that nudge our shores.
Dumb silent waves. But that
was then. Now, gentle listener,
it's time to take our leave
of Mum and Dad's proud glow, the boy's
uncertain smile. Besides,
the baby's asleep.
So let's tune out here
and slip along the dial. *Hush.*

                    Kathleen Jamie

18

'Auld wife, auld wife'

'Auld wife, auld wife,
Will ye go a-shearin?'
'Speak a wee bit looder, sir,
I'm unco dull o' hearin.'

'Auld wife, auld wife,
Wad ye tak a kiss?'
'Aye, indeed, I wull, sir;
It wadna be amiss.'

Anon.

19

Lochnagar

Away, ye gay landscapes, ye gardens of roses,
In you let the minions of luxury rove,
Restore me the rocks where the snow-flake reposes,
Though still they are sacred to freedom and love.
Yet Caledonia, beloved are thy mountains,
Round their white summits though elements war,
Though cataracts foam 'stead of smooth-flowing fountains,
I sigh for the valley of dark Lochnagar.

Ah! there my young footsteps in infancy wander'd,
My cap was the bonnet, my cloak was the plaid.
On chieftains long perish'd my memory ponder'd
As daily I strode through the pine-cover'd glade.
I sought not my home till the day's dying glory
Gave place to the rays of the bright polar star,
For fancy was cheer'd by traditional story
Disclos'd by the natives of dark Lochnagar!

Shades of the dead! Have I not heard your voices
Rise on the night-rolling breath of the gale?
Surely the soul of the hero rejoices,
And rides on the wind o'er his own Highland vale.
Round Lochnagar while the stormy mist gathers,
Winter presides in his cold icy car.
Clouds there encircle the forms of my fathers;
They dwell in the tempests of dark Lochnagar.

Ill-starr'd though brave, did no vision's foreboding
Tell you that fate had forsaken your cause?
Ah! were you destined to die at Culloden,
Victory crowned not your fall with applause.
Still were you happy in death's earthly slumber,
You rest with your clan in the caves of Braemar.
The pibroch resounds to the piper's loud number
Your deeds on the echoes of dark Lochnagar.

Years have roll'd on, Lochnagar, since I left you!
Years must elapse ere I tread you again.
Nature of verdure and flowers has bereft you,
Yet still are you dearer than Albion's plain.
England! thy beauties are tame and domestic
To one who has roved over mountains afar –
Oh! for the crags that are wild and majestic,
The steep frowning glories of dark Lochnagar.

George Gordon, Lord Byron

20

Cuddle Doon

The bairnies cuddle doon at nicht
  Wi' muckle faucht an' din –
'O, try and sleep, ye waukrife rogues,
  Your faither's comin' in' –
They never heed a word I speak;
  I try to gi'e a froon,
But aye I hap them up, an' cry,
  'O, bairnies, cuddle doon.'

Wee Jamie wi' the curly heid –
  He aye sleeps next the wa' –
Bangs up an' cries, 'I want a piece' –
  The rascal starts them a'.
I rin an' fetch them pieces, drinks,
  They stop awee the soun',
Then draw the blankets up an' cry,
  'Noo, weanies, cuddle doon.'

But ere five minutes gang, wee Rab
  Cries oot, frae 'neath the claes,
'Mither, mak' Tam gi'e ower at ance,
  He's kittling wi' his taes.'
The mischief's in that Tam for tricks,
  He'd bother half the toon;
But aye I hap them up, and cry,
  'O, bairnies, cuddle doon.'

At length they hear their faither's fit,
  An', as he steeks the door,
They turn their faces to the wa',
  While Tam pretends to snore.
'Hae a' the weans been gude?' he asks,
  As he pits aff his shoon.
'The bairnies, John, are in their beds,
  An' lang since cuddled doon.'

An' just afore we bed oorsel's,
  We look at oor wee lambs;
Tam has his airm roun' wee Rab's neck,
  An' Rab his airm roun' Tam's.
I lift wee Jamie up the bed,
  An', as I straik each croon,
I whisper, till my heart fills up,
  'O bairnies, cuddle doon.'

The bairnies cuddle doon at nicht
  Wi' mirth that's dear to me;
But sune the big warl's cark an' care
  Will quaten doon their glee.
Yet, come what will to ilka ane,
  May He who rules aboon
Aye whisper, though their pows be bald,
  'O, bairnies, cuddle doon.'

Alexander Anderson

21

The Choosing

We were first equal Mary and I –
with same-coloured ribbons in mouse-coloured hair
and with equal shyness
we curtseyed to the lady councillor
for copies of Collins' Children's Classics.
First equal, equally proud.

Best friends too Mary and I –
a common bond in being cleverest (equal)
in our small school's small class.
I remember
the competition for top desk
or to read aloud the lesson
at school service.
And my terrible fear
of her superiority at sums.

I remember the housing scheme
where we both stayed.
The same houses, different homes,
where the choices were made.

I don't know exactly why they moved,
but anyway they went.
Something about a three-apartment
and a cheaper rent.
But from the top deck of the high-school bus

I'd glimpse among the others on the corner
Mary's father, mufflered, contrasting strangely
with the elegant greyhounds by his side.
He didn't believe in high-school education,
especially for girls,
or in forking out for uniforms.

Ten years later on a Saturday –
I am coming from the library –
sitting near me on the bus,
Mary
with a husband who is tall,
curly-haired, has eyes
for no one else but Mary.
Her arms are round the full-shaped vase
that is her body.
Oh, you can see where the attraction lies
in Mary's life –
not that I envy her, really.

And I am coming from the library
with my arms full of books.
I think of those prizes that were ours for the taking
and wonder when the choices got made
we don't remember making.

Liz Lochhead

22

Kneehigh to a Poem

The way a four-year-old enters the room
By stealth to pick up a pair of, say,
Toy binoculars and looks at the wall
But really is listening to the adults

Saying nothing at all
Worth staying around for and goes:
That's how the heartbeat of a poem
Keeps us on our toes.

James McGonigal

23

Spitfires

Impossible,
to think he was once seventeen –
the man in the solid coffin,
no longer a man, no longer my grandfather, really
just a body –
too young
to serve – amazing, that he was once too young
for something – so he fixed Spitfires,
those beautiful death machines,
all Blitz pitch, all rivets.
Imagine the big wings, the heat fizz off the airfield –
taxiing a patched rig across the hardstanding
to see if she'd go –
the snubbed guns, ritzy pin-ups
on the buttressed nose.
Fighting bulldogs in their clotted greens.
He loved them seventy gentle years,
and now behind a curtain the coffin burns,
and he walks out of the hangar
in the teatime light.
He knocks his hands together once,
twice, three times. Behind him,
empty Spitfires huge as windmills
in a quiet row. He whistles,
and he's seventeen.

Claire Askew

24

Corpus Christi Carol

The heron flew east, the heron flew west,
The heron flew to the fair forest;
She flew o'er streams and meadows green
And a' to see what could be seen:
And when she saw the faithful pair,
Her breast grew sick, her head grew sair;
For there she saw a lovely bower,
Was a' clad o'er wi' lilly-flower;
And in the bower there was a bed
With silken sheets, and weel down spread,
And in the bed there lay a knight,
Whose wounds did bleed both day and night,
And by the bed there stood a stane,
And there was a' set a leal maiden,
With silver needle and silken thread,
Stemming the wounds when they did bleed.

James Hogg

25

Viewmaster

The whole world came in envelopes:
Niagara Falls in Winter,
Wild Animals of Africa,
Paris II. Useless for days,
until the machine arrived.

On the sixth day I discovered
its dated futuristic shape,
its warm brown weight,
its Belgian, Bakelite appeal.

I've always liked kinetic watches,
wind-up radios,
the manual and mechanical.
Each pull on the little lever brought
another scene to all but life:

waxworks in fifties slacks
open-mouthed at Niagara's frozen roar;

gridlock at the Arc de Triomphe;

a leopard motionless,
about to spring.

At length my arms ached like Atlas
holding the world up to a halogen sun,

feeling nearly a god,
the whole world almost in my hands.

Dorothy Lawrenson

26

Ye Cannae Shove Yer Granny Aff a Bus

Oh ye cannae shove yer granny aff a bus,
ye cannae shove yer granny aff a bus.
   Oh ye cannae shove yer granny
    fur she's yer mammy's mammy,
oh, ye cannae shove yer granny aff a bus.

Ye can shove yer other granny aff a bus,
ye can shove yer other granny aff a bus.
   Oh ye can shove yer other granny
    fur she's jist yer daddy's mammy,
oh, ye can shove yer other granny aff a bus.

Anon.

27

If Leaving You

If leaving you
was as easy
as the falling
in love
with
a
total
stranger

— not total

our blackness
a bond
before speech
or encounter

I could walk
from you now
into the hustle
and bustle
of Waverley
station
and checking
my ticket
— depart.

Maud Sulter

28

Belly-button

Lying in the bath,
I look at it, this genealogical twirl.

It connects me,
matrilineally of course,
to Morag daughter of Morag daughter of Peggy daughter of
    Catriona Mhor,
who once sailed single-handed
in a home-made canoe
between Eigg and Barra.

She was bringing home a sack of meal.

Through that severed fleshy tube
I drank my mother's poverty,
as she, in turn, had swallowed
her own mother's poverty,
and so on and so on.

The rich strawberry foam covers my starved history.

Angus Peter Campbell

29

Cross

Needling of jabs, riddle of ducks and feints,
you wait for a clear target.

It comes, as brief as a spark plug's discharge,
a flash of knicker. You unload

from the pivoting toes of the back leg,
extend through knee, hip, ribs, shoulder, elbow –

you are industrial, a piston, oiled
metal pain. Misjudge

and your attack could be countered,
your nose smacked ice pack absent numb,

worse, your blow could absorb like melt water
into the padding of your opponent's gloves.

Angela Cleland

30

To S. R. Crockett

Blows the wind to-day, and the sun and the rain are flying,
Blows the wind on the moors to-day and now,
Where about the graves of the martyrs the whaups are crying,
My heart remembers how!

Grey recumbent tombs of the dead in desert places,
Standing Stones on the vacant wine-red moor,
Hills of sheep, and the howes of the silent vanished races,
And winds, austere and pure!

Be it granted me to behold you again in dying,
Hills of home! and to hear again the call;
Hear about the graves of the martyrs the peewees crying;
And hear no more at all.

Robert Louis Stevenson

31

Tam o' Shanter: A Tale

'Of Brownyis and of Bogillis full is this buke.'
– Gawin Douglas

When chapman billies leave the street,
And drouthy neebors, neebors meet,
As market-days are wearing late,
An' folk begin to tak the gate;
While we sit bousing at the nappy,
And getting fou and unco' happy,
We think na on the lang Scots miles,
The mosses, waters, slaps and styles,
That lie between us and our hame,
Whare sits our sulky sullen dame,
Gathering her brows like gathering storm,
Nursing her wrath to keep it warm.

This truth fand honest *Tam o' Shanter*,
As he frae Ayr ae night did canter,
(Auld Ayr, wham ne'er a town surpasses,
For honest men and bonny lasses.)

O *Tam*! hadst thou but been sae wise,
As ta'en thy ain wife *Kate*'s advice!
She taul thee weel thou was a skellum,
A blethering, blustering, drunken blellum;
That frae November till October,
Ae market-day thou was nae sober;
That ilka melder, wi' the miller,
Thou sat as lang as thou had siller;
That every naig was ca'd a shoe on,

The smith and thee gat roaring fou on;
That at the L—d's house, even on Sunday,
Thou drank wi' Kirkton Jean till Monday.
She prophesied that late or soon,
Thou would be found deep drown'd in Doon;
Or catch'd wi' warlocks in the mirk,
By *Alloway*'s auld haunted kirk.

Ah, gentle dames! it gars me greet,
To think how mony counsels sweet,
How mony lengthen'd sage advices,
The husband frae the wife despises!

But to our tale: Ae market-night,
Tam had got planted unco right;
Fast by an ingle, bleezing finely,
Wi' reaming swats, that drank divinely;
And at his elbow, Souter *Johnny*,
His ancient, trusty, drouthy crony;
Tam lo'ed him like a vera brither;
The had been fou for weeks thegither.
The night drave on wi' sangs and clatter;
And ay the ale was growing better:
The landlady and *Tam* grew gracious,
Wi' favours, secret, sweet, and precious:
The Souter tauld his queerest stories;
The landlord's laugh was ready chorus:
The storm without might rair and rustle,
Tam did na mind the storm a whistle.

Care, mad to see a man sae happy,
E'en drown'd himsel amang the nappy:

As bees flee hame wi' lades o' treasure,
The minutes wing'd their way wi' pleasure;
Kings may be blest, but *Tam* was glorious,
O'er a' the ills o' life victorious!

  But pleasures are like poppies spread,
You seize the flower, its bloom is shed;
Or like the snow falls in the river,
A moment white – then melts for ever;
Or like the borealis race,
That flit ere you can point their place;
Or like the rainbow's lovely form
Evanishing amid the storm. –
Nae man can tether time or tide;
The hour approaches *Tam* maun ride;
That hour, o' night's black arch the key-stane,
That dreary hour he mounts his beast in;
And sic a night he taks the road in,
As ne'er poor sinner was abroad in.

  The wind blew as 'twad blawn its last;
The rattling showers rose on the blast;
The speedy gleams the darkness swallow'd;
Loud, deep, and lang, the thunder bellow'd:
That night, a child might understand,
The Deil had business on his hand.

  Weel mounted on his gray mare, *Meg*,
A better never lifted leg,
Tam skelpit on thro' dub and mire,
Despising wind, and rain, and fire;
Whiles holding fast his gude blue bonnet;

Whiles crooning o'er some auld Scots sonnet;
Whiles glowring round wi' prudent cares,
Lest bogles catch him unawares:
Kirk-Alloway was drawing nigh,
Whare ghaists and houlets nightly cry. –

  By this time he was cross the ford,
Whare, in the snaw, the chapman smoor'd;
And past the birks and meikle stane,
Whare drunken *Charlie* brak's neck-bane;
And thro' the whins, and by the cairn,
Whare hunters fand the murder'd bairn;
And near the thorn, aboon the well,
Whare *Mungo*'s mither hang'd hersel. –
Before him *Doon* pours all his floods;
The doubling storm roars thro' the woods;
The lightnings flash from pole to pole;
Near and more near the thunders roll:
When, glimmering thro' the groaning trees,
Kirk-Alloway seem'd in a bleeze;
Thro' ilka bore the beams were glancing;
And loud resounded mirth and dancing. –

  Inspiring bold *John Barleycorn*!
What dangers thou canst make us scorn!
Wi' tippeny, we fear nae evil;
Wi' usquabae, we'll face the devil! –
The swats sae ream'd in *Tammie*'s noddle,
Fair play, he car'd na deils a boddle.
But *Maggie* stood right sair astonish'd,
Till, by the heel and hand admonish'd,
She ventured forward on the light;

And, vow! *Tam* saw an unco sight!
Warlocks and witches in a dance;
Nae cotillion brent new frae *France*,
But hornpipes, jigs, strathspeys, and reels,
Put life and mettle in their heels.
A winnock-bunker in the east,
There sat auld Nick, in shape o' beast;
A towzie tyke, black, grim, and large,
To gie them music was his charge:
He screw'd the pipes and gart them skirl,
Till roof and rafters a' did dirl. –
Coffins stood round, like open presses,
That shaw'd the dead in their last dresses;
And by some devilish cantraip slight
Each in its cauld hand held a light. –
By which heroic *Tam* was able
To note upon the haly table,
A murderer's banes in gibbet airns;
Twa span-lang, wee, unchristen'd bairns;
A thief, new-cutted frae a rape,
Wi' his last gasp his gab did gape;
Five tomahawks, wi' blude red-rusted;
Five scymitars, wi' murder crusted;
A garter, which a babe had strangled;
A knife, a father's throat had mangled,
Whom his ain son o' life bereft,
The grey hairs yet stack to the heft;
Wi' mair o' horrible and awefu',
Which even to name wad be unlawfu'.

As *Tammie* glow'rd, amaz'd, and curious,
The mirth and fun grew fast and furious:

The piper loud and louder blew;
The dancers quick and quicker flew;
They reel'd, they set, they cross'd, they cleekit,
Till ilka carlin swat and reekit,
And coost her duddies to the wark,
And linket at it in her sark!

Now, *Tam*, O *Tam*! had thae been queans,
A' plump and strapping in their teens,
Their sarks, instead o' creeshie flannen,
Been snaw-white seventeen hunder linnen!
Thir breeks o' mine, my only pair,
That ance were plush, o' gude blue hair,
I wad hae gi'en them off my hurdies,
For ae blink o' the bonie burdies!

But wither'd beldams, auld and droll,
Rigwoodie hags wad spean a foal,
Lowping and flinging on a crummock,
I wonder didna turn thy stomach.

But *Tam* kend what was what fu' brawlie,
There was ae winsome wench and wawlie,
That night enlisted in the core,
(Lang after kend on *Carrick* shore;
For mony a beast to dead she shot,
And perish'd mony a bony boat,
And shook baith meikle corn and bear,
And kept the country-side in fear:)
Her cutty sark, o' Paisley harn,
That while a lassie she had worn,
In longitude tho' sorely scanty,

It was her best, and she was vauntie. –
Ah! little kend thy reverend grannie,
That sark she coft for her wee Nannie,
Wi' twa pund Scots, ('twas a' her riches),
Wad ever grac'd a dance of witches!

But here my Muse her wing maun cour;
Sic flights are far beyond her pow'r;
To sing how Nannie lap and flang,
(A souple jade she was, and strang),
And how *Tam* stood, like ane bewitch'd,
And thought his very een enrich'd;
Even Satan glowr'd, and fidg'd fu' fain,
And hotch'd an blew wi' might and main:
Till first ae caper, syne anither,
Tam tint his reason a' thegither,
And roars out, 'Weel done, Cutty-sark!'
And in an instant all was dark:
And scarcely had he Maggie rallied.
When out the hellish legion sallied.

As bees bizz out wi' angry fyke,
When plundering herds assail their byke;
As open pussie's mortal foes,
When, pop! she starts before their nose;
As eager runs the market-crowd,
When 'Catch the thief!' resounds aloud;
So Maggie runs, the witches follow,
Wi' mony an eldritch skreech and hollow.

Ah, *Tam*! Ah, *Tam*! thou'll get thy fairin!
In hell they'll roast thee like a herrin!

In vain thy *Kate* awaits thy comin!
Kate soon will be a woefu' woman!
Now, do thy speedy utmost, Meg,
And win the key-stane of the brig;
There at them thou thy tail may toss,
A running stream they dare na cross.
But ere the key-stane she could make,
The fient a tail she had to shake!
For Nannie, far before the rest,
Hard upon noble Maggie prest,
And flew at *Tam* wi' furious ettle;
But little wist she Maggie's mettle –
Ae spring brought off her master hale,
But left behind her ain gray tail:
The carlin claught her by the rump,
And left poor Maggie scarce a stump.

Now, wha this tale o' truth shall read,
Ilk man and mother's son, take heed:
Whene'er to drink you are inclin'd,
Or cutty-sarks run in your mind,
Think, ye may buy the joys o'er dear,
Remember Tam o' Shanter's mare.

Robert Burns

November

I

For as Long as

For as long
As the sun appears
And disappears
In whichever whatever way
And the moon and stars
Blink and shine
With Jupiter in the evening sky
Here we live
And here we die.

Alan Young

2

St Martin's Summer

As swallows turning backward
    When half-way o'er the sea,
At one word's trumpet summons
    They came again to me –
The hopes I had forgotten
    Came back again to me.

I know not which to credit,
    O lady of my heart!
Your eyes that bade me linger,
    Your words that bade us part –
I know not which to credit,
    My reason or my heart.

But be my hopes rewarded,
    Or be they but in vain,
I have dreamed a golden vision,
    I have gathered in the grain –
I have dreamed a golden vision,
    I have not lived in vain.

Robert Louis Stevenson

3

Skye lines

I
a stone – a rock
a single track

an aird – a stack
a dolphin's back

Hallaig – a cairn
a cataract

Sorley MacLean
into the main

II
a cliff – a drop
a long way down

a dun – a broch
a long road home

a fence – a gull
a scallop shell

a coral beach
a pilgrimage

a Cuillin view
a ringing rock

a scarp – a loch
a sunset too

III
harbour – heron
the *Bella Jane*

small lights in boats
jetty – a float

a castle – a keep
sheer drop – steep

a lover's leap
a fishing fleet

IV

a four-winged isle
a daffodil

Trotternish
a splash – a fish

burning heather
passing places

the weather, the *weather*
silence, spaces

a bridge – a sound
a tide – a tor

a wave – a shore
a harbinger

Patricia Ace

4

Love Poem

The ways will never part
for us, I tell you now.
I write this in November
among the autumn leaves
the masks of Halloween,
that red Remembrance day.

We have had too much frost
and high snow together.
It is time for us to say;
This ring which once was salt
breeds blossoms round the bone,
and a whole life's union.

The sea stormy above
is always calm beneath.
The anchor will still hold
though the yachts dance and froth
in tantrums near the shore,
their masts like matchsticks.

For though it's autumn now
the trees will soon put on
their green crowns once more
as we too shall do
however weasels hunt
in the thick undergrowth.

Dear girl in your white muffs
and your red coat, I swear
no gaunt wolf from my heart
shall ever eat you up
except through love alone,
through love's most devious ways

and we two, hand in hand,
shall walk through all the mirrors
unsplintered to the end,
till only the bones remain
to stand up in all weathers
under the haunting wind.

Iain Crichton Smith

5

Fireworks aff the Castle

Fireworks aff the Castle
Goin WHEECH, WHEECH, WHEECH
Bairns in the library
Gettin WHEESHT, WHEESHT, WHEESHT

Cans o Irn Bru
Goin SKOOSHITAY, SKOOSHITAY, SKOOSH
Fitbaw in the playgroond
Gettin DOOSHITAY, DOOSHITAY, DOOSH

The snaw blaws in fae Norroway
And nips your TAES, TAES, TAES
We go skitin on wir sledges
Doon the BRAES, BRAES, BRAES

The rain comes doon in buckets
And it's WEET, WEET, WEET
Your teeth is sair fae sweeties
And it's GREET, GREET, GREET

You're oot wi pals and aw the time
It's BLETHER, BLETHER, BLETHER
But when awthin's wrang and no goin right
Jist go and tell your MITHER
When awthin's wrang and no goin right
Jist you coorie in wi MITHER

Matthew Fitt

6

Almorness

The tide is sidling up to Almorness,
unmet by those returned now north & west
away from here, back to the daily grind
of mornings, work & dinner, closing time
& mornings. Just a couple & three dogs on
White Horse Beach, grey haired, their many stops
a hint of winter in this cusp of days
when everything's retreating to a place
less friendly & exposed. November starts
to pull on thicker drawers & warmer clothes

Stuart A. Paterson

7

In the Gallery: Portrait of a Lady (Unknown)

Veiled eyes, yet quick to meet one glance
Not his, not yours, but *mine*,
Lips that are fain to stir and breathe
Dead joys (not love nor wine):
'Tis not in *you* the secret lurks
That makes men pause and pass!

Did unseen magic flow from you
Long since to madden hearts,
And those who loathed remain to pray
And work their dolorous parts –
To seek your riddle, dread or sweet,
And find it in the grave?

Till someone painted you one day,
Perchance to ease his soul.
And set you here to weave your spells
While time and silence roll;
And you were hungry for the hour
When one should understand?

Your jewelled fingers writhe and gleam
From out your sombre vest;
Am I the first of those who gaze,
Who may their meaning guess,
Yet dare not whisper lest the words
Pale even painted cheeks?

Katharine de Mattos

8

Windy Nights

Whenever the moon and stars are set,
   Whenever the wind is high,
All night long in the dark and wet,
   A man goes riding by.
Late in the night when the fires are out,
Why does he gallop and gallop about?

Whenever the trees are crying aloud,
   And ships are tossed at sea,
By, on the highway, low and loud,
   By at the gallop goes he.
By at the gallop he goes, and then
By he comes back at the gallop again.

Robert Louis Stevenson

9

The Work

If I have to, then let me be *the whaler poet*,
launcher of the knife, portioning off
the pink cut, salt trim and fat, tipping
the larger waste off the side of the boat,
and then to have the poem in the drawer;

or, perhaps, let it be *the poet nurse*,
hearts measured by a small watch, balmer,
washer of old skin, stopping by the door
in the night –
                    or *the oil-driller poet*, primed
for the buried flame and heat, lips to the black,

aware how the oilfields in the evening
are lit like our own staggered desks.
Or, *the horse-trader* or *the smith*, or *the waiter poet* –
offering the choice wine, polishing to the light,
the bringer of the feast and the bill.

                                        Niall Campbell

10

Gaelic Blessing

from Carmina Gadelica

Beannachd Dhè a bhith agaibh,
'S guma math a dh'èireas dhuibh;
Beannachd Chriosda a bhith agaibh,
'S guma math a chuirear ruibh;
Beannachd Spioraid a bhith agaibh,
'S guma math a chuireas sibh seachad bhur saoghal,
Gach latha dh'èireas sibh a suas,
Gath oidhche laigheas sibh a slos.

God's blessing be yours,
and well may it befall you;
Christ's blessing be yours,
And well be you entreated;
Spirit's blessing be yours,
And well spend you your lives,
Each day that you rise up,
Each night that you lie down.

Anon.,
translated by Alexander Carmichael

11

When You See Millions of the Mouthless Dead

When you see millions of the mouthless dead
Across your dreams in pale battalions go,
Say not soft things as other men have said,
That you'll remember. For you need not so.
Give them not praise. For, deaf, how should they know
It is not curses heaped on each gashed head?
Nor tears. Their blind eyes see not your tears flow.
Nor honour. It is easy to be dead.
Say only this, 'They are dead.' Then add thereto,
'Yet many a better one has died before.'
Then, scanning all the o'ercrowded mass, should you
Perceive one face that you loved heretofore,
It is a spook. None wears the face you knew.
Great death has made all his for evermore.

Charles Hamilton Sorley

12

Shh . . .

they found me in the corner
way at the back
of my mother's wardrobe

at first they thought i was a button
broken loose from a frayed thread
or a mothball, happy in the dark

then, as i grew, they thought i was
a shoe without a partner, but
they were busy folk – it was easier
to poke me back beside the fallen
jumpers and the missing socks

as for me, i was quite content
tucked up in the folds of mother's frocks

from time to time she'd drag me out
wear me, dangled prettily
on the end of her arm –
the ultimate accessory
a quiet daughter

Magi Gibson

13

Vault

after Marion Coutts, 'For the Fallen'

And just when we thought, when we thought, when we thought
We could not   we could not
We did, we did   we leapt, we leapt
We made it   across, across.
We fell often   were broken; we lost.
The past is a leap   in the dark: a dark horse.
We laughed. We wept. Of course, of course.

Jackie Kay

14

November Night, Edinburgh

The night tinkles like ice in glasses.
Leaves are glued to the pavements with frost.
The brown air fumes at the shop windows,
Tries the door, and sidles past.

I gulp down winter raw. The heady
Darkness swirls with tenements.
In a brown fuzz of cottonwool
Lamps fade up crags, die into pits.

Frost in my lungs is harsh as leaves
Scraped up on paths. – I look up, there,
A high roof sails, at the mast-head
Fluttering a grey and ragged star.

The world's a bear shrugged in his den.
It's snug and close in the snoring night.
And outside like chrysanthemums
The fog unfolds its bitter scent.

Norman MacCaig

15

Saint Margaret

Born Hungary, 1045, died Edinburgh, 1093; married to King
Malcolm III – Ceann Mòr / Canmore; the only royal Scottish Saint,
known as the Pearl of Scotland, but among the Gaels as 'Maighread
nam Mallachd'.

There was luck in it that day,
we thought, good fortune rising for us,
though an accident, they say:
taken by storm, she was – twice –
first at sea, driven to our shore,
then at the king's heart: Ceann Mòr
just *had* to have her for his queen.

She came from two lands – one we didn't know,
far to the East, the other we did – too well.
Cho brèagha, was the whisper of the court,
this woman more fair than any we had seen,
pale as the pearls I clasped around
her slender neck at dawn each day,
jewelled fingers spooning warm *brochan*
into blue-lipped orphan mouths
by the palace door at sunrise –
always before she broke fast herself –
giving forever on her mind.

She bore our land a line of kings,
gave us Queensferry for the pilgrims,
miracles, peace and constant prayer,
swept change through the old church
with the lovely lustre of her Roman rites.
So proud of her, our king, who couldn't read,
he had her books encased with gems and woven gold
in praise of her refinement; she held the key to heaven,
he said, and to the labour of our earthly days,
his court's guiding star in this tale of new ways
told in English from that hour she wore the crown;
for he charged us all to speak her language,
put her at ease, and willingly we did.

And now she rests with him in our Saviour's arms.
I miss her quiet radiance that filled the years.
I walked to her cave today, down by the river Ferm –
her place of solitude and contemplation;
I thought to thank her in prayer – and here's a thing:
standing there alone in that womb of rock, I yearned
for the old tongue my mother learned me on her lap,
words that once rose up from deep inside me;
but they're lost, the well is dry – it's like a fatal thirst
that can't be quenched; and I know now why
my mother called her Margaret the Accursed.

Gerda Stevenson

16

Anthem

In my disorder I shivered sweated, yawned
with fear and wrote some lines that went beyond
wit's end. We travelled south. We hadn't planned
on coming north again and buying this land
of little things where dwarf ferns unfurl their fronds,
newts and frogs come back to the garden pond,
a mistle thrush sings before the day has dawned.

Yes – any how-when-where by drop-dead chance.
And so I've been rehearsing final things
for years. I've bought my ashes in advance.
Until that harvesting
I'll observe the natural ordinance
of fern and newt and frog and a thrush that sings
the anthem in my land of little things.

James Aitchison

17

Prayer

Some days, although we cannot pray, a prayer
utters itself. So, a woman will lift
her head from the sieve of her hands and stare
at the minims sung by a tree, a sudden gift.

Some nights, although we are faithless, the truth
enters our hearts, that small familiar pain;
then a man will stand stock-still, hearing his youth
in the distant Latin chanting of a train.

Pray for us now. Grade I piano scales
console the lodger looking out across
a Midlands town. Then dusk, and someone calls
a child's name as though they named their loss.

Darkness outside. Inside, the radio's prayer –
Rockall. Malin. Dogger. Finisterre.

Carol Ann Duffy

18

Taal

This music will not sit in straight lines.
The notes refuse to perch on wires

but move in rhythm with the dancer
round the face of the clock,
through the dandelion head of time.

We feel blown free, but circle back
to be in love, to touch and part
and meet again, spun

past the face of the moon, the precise
underpinning of stars. The cycle begins
with one and ends with one,

dha dhin dhin dha. There must be
other feet in step with us, an underbeat,
a voice that keeps count, not yours or mine.

This music is playing us.
We are playing with time.

Imtiaz Dharker

19

Lord Ullin's Daughter

A chieftain to the Highlands bound,
Cries, 'Boatman, do not tarry;
And I'll give thee a silver pound
To row us o'er the ferry.'

'Now who be ye would cross Lochgyle,
This dark and stormy water?'
'Oh, I'm the chief of Ulva's isle
And this Lord Ullin's daughter.

'And fast before her father's men
Three days we've fled together,
For should he find us in the glen,
My blood would stain the heather.

'His horsemen hard behind us ride;
Should they our steps discover,
Then who will cheer my bonny bride
When they have slain her lover?'

Out spoke the hardy Highland wight:
'I'll go, my chief – I'm ready:
It is not for your silver bright
But for your winsome lady.

'And by my word, the bonny bird
In danger shall not tarry;
So though the waves are raging white
I'll row you o'er the ferry.'

By this the storm grew loud apace,
The water-wraith was shrieking;
And in the scowl of heaven each face
Grew dark as they were speaking.

But still, as wilder grew the wind,
And as the night grew drearer,
A-down the glen rode armèd men –
Their tramping sounded nearer.

'O haste thee, haste!' the lady cries,
'Though tempests round us gather;
I'll meet the raging of the skies,
But not an angry father.'

The boat has left a stormy land,
A stormy sea before her –
When oh! too strong for human hand
The tempest gathered o'er her.

And still they rowed amidst the roar
Of waters fast prevailing;
Lord Ullin reached that fatal shore –
His wrath was changed to wailing.

For sore dismay'd, through storm and shade,
His child he did discover;
One lovely hand was stretched for aid,
And one was round her lover.

'Come back! come back!' he cried in grief,
'Across this stormy water;
And I'll forgive your Highland chief,
My daughter! – oh, my daughter!'

'Twas vain: the loud waves lashed the shore,
Return or aid preventing;
The waters wild went o'er his child,
And he was left lamenting.

Thomas Campbell

20

Churning Charm

Come, butter, come,
Come, butter, come!
Peter stauns at the gate,
Waitin for a buttered cake.
Come, butter, come!

Anon.

Canadian Boat Song

Listen to me, as when you heard our fathers
Sing long ago the song of other shores –
Listen to me, and then in chorus gather
All your deep voices, as ye pull your oars.

Chorus
    Fair these broad meads – these hoary woods are grand;
    But we are exiles from our fathers' land.

From the lone sheiling of the misty island
Mountains divide us, and the waste of seas –
Yet still the blood is strong, the heart is Highland,
And we in dreams behold the Hebrides.

Chorus

We ne'er shall tread the fancy-haunted valley,
Where 'tween the dark hills creeps the small clear stream,
In arms around the patriarch banner rally,
Nor see the moon on royal tombstones gleam.

Chorus

When the bold kindred, in the time long vanish'd,
Conquered the soil and fortified the keep –
No seer foretold the children would be banish'd
That a degenerate lord might boast his sheep.

Chorus

Come foreign rage – let Discord burst in slaughter!
O then for clansmen true, and stern claymore –
The hearts that would have given their blood like water
Beat heavily beyond the Atlantic roar.

Anon.

22

Sir Patrick Spens

The king sits in Dumfermline toun,
    Drinking the blood-reid wine:
'O whaur will I get skeely skipper,
    To sail this new ship of mine?'

An' up and spake an eldern knicht,
    Sat at the kings richt knee:
'Sir Patrick Spens is the best sailor
    That ever sail'd the sea.'

The king has written a braid letter,
    And sealed it wi' his hand,
And sent it to Sir Patrick Spens,
    Was walking on the strand.

'To Noroway, to Noroway
    To Noroway o'er the faem,
The king's dauchter of Noroway,
    'Tis thou maun bring her hame.'

The first line that Sir Patrick read,
    So loud, loud lauched he;
The neist line that Sir Patrick read.
    The tear blinded his ee.

'O wha is this has done this deid,
    This ill deid done to me,
To send me out this time o' the year,
    To sail upon the sea?

'Be it wind, be it weet, be it hail, be it sleet,
    Our ship maun sail the faem;
The king's daughter o' Noroway,
    'Tis we maun fetch her hame.'

They hoysed their sails on Monenday morn,
    Wi a' the speed they may;
They hae landed in Noroway,
    Upon a Wodensday.

They hadna been a week, a week
    In Noroway but twae,
When that the lords o' Noroway
    Began aloud to say:

'Ye Scottishmen spend a' our king's goud,
    And a' our queenis fee!'
'Ye lie, ye lie, ye liars loud,
    Sae loud I hear ye lie!

'For I hae brought as much o' the white money
    As gane my men and me,
And I brought a half fou o' gude red goud
    Oot o'er the sea wi' me.

'Mak ready, mak ready, my merry men a',
    Our gude ship sails the morn.'
'Now ever alack, my maister dear,
    For I fear a deadly storm.

'I saw the new mune late yestreen,
    Wi the auld mune in her arm,
And I fear, I fear, my maister dear,
    That we will come to harm.'

They hadna sailed a league, a league,
    A league but barely three,
When the lift grew dark, and the wind blew loud,
    And gurly grew the sea.

The ankers brak, and the tapmasts lap,
    It was sic a deidly storm,
And the waves came o'er the broken ship,
    Till a' her sides were torn.

'O whaur will I get a gude sailor,
    To tak the helm in hand,
Till I get up to the tall tapmast,
    To see if I can spy land?'

'O here am I, a sailor gude,
    To tak the helm in hand,
Till you go up to the tall tapmast;
    But I fear you'll ne'er spy land.'

He hadna gane a step, a step,
    A step but barely ane,
When a bout flew out of our goodly ship,
    And the saut sea it cam in.

'Gae fetch a web o' the silken claith,
    Anither o' the twine,
And wap them into our gude ship's side,
    And let na the sea come in.'

They fetched a web o' the silken claith,
    Anither o' the twine,
And they wapped them into that gude ship's side,
    But still the sea cam in.

O laith, laith were our gude Scots lords
    To weet their cork-heeled shoon;
But lang or a' the play was played,
    They wat their hats aboon.

And mony was the feather-bed
    That flottered on the faem,
And mony was the gude lord's son
    That never mair cam hame.

O lang, lang may the ladies sit,
    Wi their fans intil their hand,
Or eir they see Sir Patrick Spens
    Cum sailing to the land.

O lang, lang may the maidens sit,
    Wi their gowd kames in their hair,
Waiting for their ain deir lords,
    For them they'll see nay mair.

Half owre, half owre to Aberdour,
    'Tïs fiftie fadom deip,
And thair lies guid Sir Patrick Spens,
    Wi the Scots lords at his feit.

Anon.

23

To a Mouse

On turning her up in her nest with the plough,
November 1785

Wee, sleekit, cowrin, tim'rous beastie,
O, what a panic's in thy breastie!
Thou need na start awa sae hasty,
    Wi' bickerin brattle!
I wad be laith to rin an' chase thee
    Wi' murd'ring pattle!

I'm truly sorry Man's dominion
Has broken Nature's social union,
An' justifies that ill opinion,
    Which makes thee startle,
At me, thy poor, earth-born companion,
    An' fellow-mortal!

I doubt na, whyles, but thou may thieve;
What then? poor beastie, thou maun live!
A daimen-icker in a thrave
    'S a sma' request:
I'll get a blessin wi' the lave,
    An' never miss 't!

Thy wee-bit housie, too, in ruin!
It's silly wa's the win's are strewin!
An' naething, now, to big a new ane,
   O' foggage green!
An' bleak December's winds ensuin,
    Baith snell an' keen!

Thou saw the fields laid bare an' waste,
An' weary Winter comin fast,
An' cozie here, beneath the blast,
   Thou thought to dwell,
Till crash! the cruel coulter past
    Out thro' thy cell.

That wee-bit heap o' leaves an' stibble
Has cost thee monie a weary nibble!
Now thou's turn'd out, for a' thy trouble,
   But house or hald,
To thole the Winter's sleety dribble,
    An' cranreuch cauld!

But Mousie, thou art no thy-lane,
In proving foresight may be vain:
The best laid schemes o' Mice an' Men
   Gang aft agley,
An' lea'e us nought but grief an' pain,
    For promis'd joy!

Still, thou art blest, compar'd wi' me!
The present only toucheth thee:
But Och! I backward cast my e'e,
    On prospects drear!
An' forward tho' I canna see,
    I guess an' fear!

Robert Burns

24

The Poacher to Orion

November-month is wearin by,
The leaves is nearly doon;
I watch ye stride alang the sky
O nichts, my beltit loon.

The treetaps wi their fingers bare
Spread between me and you,
But weel in yonder frosty air
Ye see me keekin through.

At schule I lairnd richt wearilie
The Hunter was yer name;
Sma pleasure were ye then tae me,
But noo oor trade's the same.

But ye've a brawer job nor mine
And better luck nor me,
For them that sees ye likes ye fine
And the pollis lets ye be.

We're baith astir when men's asleep;
A hunter aye pursued,
I hae by dyke an ditch tae creep,
But ye gang safe an prood.

What maitter that? I'll no complain,
For when we twa are met
We hae the nicht-watch for oor ain
Till the stars are like tae set.

Gang on, my lad. The warlds owreheid
Wheel on their nichtly beat,
And ye'll mind ye as the skies ye treid
O the brither at yer feet.

Violet Jacob

25

from Dance tae yer daddy

Dance tae yer daddy,
Ma bonnie laddie,
Dance tae yer daddy, ma bonnie lamb!
An ye'll get a fishie
In a little dishie,
Ye'll get a fishie, whan the boat comes hame.

Anon.

26

Constant, Constant, Little Light

A twenty-first-century version of Jane Taylor's poem
'The Star', now universally known as the nursery rhyme
'Twinkle, Twinkle Little Star'.

Constant, constant, little light,
catch my eye in darkest night.
What can speed so fast, so high,
laser-like across the sky?

When the sleepy sun has set
and the night has cast her net,
It's then your orbit forms a ring,
round the earth a song to sing.

Constant, constant, little light,
I know you're a satellite.

Cruising, spinning, seldom seen,
beaming pictures to our screens.
Weather-watching, tracking storms,
plotting maps and all life forms.

Scanning, spying from above,
are you hawk or are you dove?
Silent, stealthy space-age Thor,
armed with weapons for a real star war.

From your tiny, silver glow,
who can tell what wrongs may flow?
But for now I hold you bright,
constant, constant, little light.

Constant, constant, little light,
I know you're a satellite.

John Rice

27

Mousie, mousie, come tae me

Mousie, mousie, come tae me,
The cat's awa frae hame;
Mousie, come tae me,
I'll use ye kind, an mak ye tame.

Anon.

28

John Frost

You've come early to see us this year, John Frost,
Wi' your crispin' an' poutherin' gear, John Frost,
    For hedge, tower, an' tree,
    As far as I see,
Are as white as the bloom o' the pear, John Frost.

You're very preceese wi' your wark, John Frost!
Altho' ye ha'e wrought in the dark, John Frost,
    For ilka fit-stap,
    Frae the door to the slap,
Is braw as a new linen sark, John Frost.

There are some things about ye I like, John Frost,
And ithers that aft gar me fyke, John Frost;
    For the weans, wi' cauld taes,
    Crying 'shoon, stockings, claes,'
Keep us busy as bees in the byke, John Frost.

And gae 'wa' wi' your lang slides, I beg, John Frost!
Bairn's banes are as bruckle's an egg, John Frost;
    For a cloit o' a fa'
    Gars them hirple awa',
Like a hen wi' a happity leg, John Frost.

Ye ha'e fine goings on in the north, John Frost!
Wi' your houses o' ice and so forth, John Frost!
 Tho' their kirn's on the fire,
 They may kirn till they tire,
Yet their butter – pray what is it worth, John Frost?

Now, your breath would be greatly improven, John Frost,
By a scone pipin'-het frae the oven, John Frost;
 And your blae frosty nose
 Nae beauty wad lose,
Kent ye mair baith o' boiling and stovin', John Frost.

William Miller

29

Luss Village

Such walls, like honey, and the old are happy
in morphean air like gold-fish in a bowl.
Ripe roses trail their margins down a sleepy
mediaeval treatise on the slumbering soul.

And even the water, fabulously silent,
has no salt tales to tell us, nor makes jokes
about the yokel mountains, huge and patient,
that will not court her but read shadowy books.

A world so long departed! In the churchyard
the tilted tombs still gossip, and the leaves
of stony testaments are read by Richard,
Jean and Carol, pert among the sheaves

of unscythed shadows, while the noon day hums
with bees and water and the ghosts of psalms.

Iain Crichton Smith

30

Harp of the North, Farewell!

Harp of the North, farewell! The hills grow dark,
　On purple peaks a deeper shade descending;
In twilight copse the glow-worm lights her spark,
　The deer, half-seen, are to the covert wending.
Resume thy wizard elm! the fountain lending,
　And the wild breeze, thy wilder minstrelsy;
Thy numbers sweet with nature's vespers blending,
　With distant echo from the fold and lea,
And herd-boy's evening pipe, and hum of housing bee.

Yet once again farewell, thou Minstrel harp!
　Yet once again forgive my feeble sway,
And little reck I of the censure sharp
　May idly cavil at an idle lay.
Much have I owed thy strains on life's long way,
　Through secret woes the world has never known,
When on the weary night dawned wearier day,
　And bitterer was the grief devoured alone.
That I o'erlived such woes, Enchantress! is thine own.

Hark! as my lingering footsteps slow retire,
　　Some Spirit of the Air has waked thy string!
'Tis now a seraph bold, with touch of fire,
　　'Tis now the brush of Fairy's frolic wing.
Receding now, the dying numbers ring
　　Fainter and fainter down the rugged dell,
And now the mountain breezes scarcely bring
　　A wandering witch-note of the distant spell –
And now, 'tis silent all! – Enchantress, fare thee well!

Sir Walter Scott

December

I

The Road and the Miles to Dundee

Cauld winter was howlin o'er moor and o'er mountain
And wild was the surge of the dark rolling sea,
When I met about daybreak a bonnie young lassie
Wha asked me the road and the miles to Dundee.

Says I, 'My young lassie, I canna weel tell ye,
The road and the distance I canna weel gie.
But if ye'll permit me tae gang a wee bittie,
I'll show ye the road and the miles to Dundee.'

At once she consentit and gave me her airm,
Ne'er a word did I speir wha the lassie micht be,
She appeared like an angel in feature and form,
As she walked by my side on the road to Dundee.

At length wi the Howe o Strathmartine behind us,
The spires o the toun in full view we could see,
Said she, 'Gentle sir, I can never forget ye
For showing me far on the road to Dundee.'

I took the gowd pin from the scarf on my bosom
And said, 'Keep ye this in remembrance o me.'
Then bravely I kissed the sweet lips o the lassie,
E'er I parted wi her on the road to Dundee.

So here's to the lassie, I ne'er can forget her,
And ilka young laddie that's list'ning to me,
O never be sweer to convoy a young lassie
Though it's only to show her the road to Dundee.

Anon.

2

It's the Sea I Want

It's the sea I want,
Make no mistake,
Not the resorts
With boardinghouses
Pressed together and shivering,
Praying for sun
And central heating –
It's the sea I want,
The whole boiling,
Destructive, disruptive, sterilising –
I think it's smashing

Undermining
This island,
Unpinning
Gorse and headland,
Arresting, without warrant,
Growth and sunlight.
Landscapes at risk,
Thumped with fists of wind,
Eaten up with a mouthful of mist,
Slump like a Stock Market
Suddenly into the Channel.
Down the long final slide
Go houses full of the dying,
Carefully tended gardens
Into the riot of salt . . .

While
All along
A population of cold
Shelled and speechless creatures
Waits, to inherit
The hot, hideous, restless
Chaos I've helped to make
In sixty industrious years.
Sixty industrious years
And the motorway from the Midlands
Have brought me down at last
To the level of the sea.
I see with the sea's eye.

It bites the cliffs,
Fondles the coast, and swings
Away again, out to sea,
Waving, waving,
Making no promises,
It spits back in our faces
The coins and cans of the beaches.

It's the sea I want,
Belting the land, breaking
All the rules, speaking
Its guttural, thrusting tongue.
It pays no taxes,
Cringes before no conscience
And carries its own prestige
On its naked, shining back.

It's the sea I want,
If it's not too late
To sit, and contemplate
The hard bright barbarous jewels
Of the totally indifferent sea:
Something I never made
And cannot be guilty of.

I have done with the pains of love.
Leave me alone with the sea,
That picks bones clean,
And was, and shall be.

Elma Mitchell

3

Stars

Wish upon
Follow your
This is the one
The Wise Men saw
Near and far
What we are

Thank your lucky
Catch a falling
You might be struck
Or like to swing

The night has a thousand
In the bright sky
In the ascendant
To steer your life by

Hitch your wagon
Hunt Orion
Born to wander
Following yonder

O little
O twinkle twinkle

Hamish Whyte and
Diana Hendry

4

December Day

I ask no lovelier thing
Than this December silver:
See how the light flakes off the new-turned plough
Under the slow great swing
Of branches, silver-boled;
Not all the silken, tender ways of spring
Can over-pass this cold
And windy beauty; see
Where thin-blown ripples spreading
Pattern the water with a mesh of gold.
Not war, nor present misery,
Can rout earth's ageless peace
Or check the steady rhythm of her soil
To yield and year's increase.
Yet sun in earth, yet love in man works on,
And shall not cease.

Dorothy Margaret Paulin

5

Winter

In rigorous hours, when down the iron lane
The redbreast looks in vain
For hips and haws,
Lo, shining flowers upon my window pane
The silver pencil of the winter draws.

When all the snowy hill
And the bare woods are still;
When snipes are silent in the frozen bogs,
And all the garden garth is whelmed in mire,
Lo, by the hearth, the laughter of the logs –
More fair than roses, lo, the flowers of fire!

Robert Louis Stevenson

6

Looking west

I dream we are two Viking jarls today,
with simple action plans and strategies –
along the lines of take life by the throat;
travelling in thrall into high places
spying out these wide Hesperides

from Skye's blue jagged Cuillin
to Jura's rounded paps, Kintyre
and even far-off Arran's hazy peaks
and all the lateral wonders
of a world adjacent and between
the blest islands of the west:
Iona, Colonsay, Coll
and Tiree, the Uists,
Barra, Mingulay,
stretching into the blue,
with Staffa, Ulva, Eorsa nearer to
our vantage point of Mull's Ben More.

This summit is among the high points
of two lives. Mind how you go,
you two. Evade descent.
Postpone the parting handclasp.
Consider another golden moment
and reflect. Beyond this pinnacle
a setting sun declines
into the anecdotage of Valhalla
and the sea. For every thing
that rises has to ebb.

Gordon Jarvie

7

Ma plaid awa, ma plaid awa

Ma plaid awa, ma plaid awa,
An ower the hill an faur awa,
An faur awa tae Norrowa,
Ma plaid sall no be blawn awa!
 The elfin knicht sits on yon hill,
  Ba, ba, bella ba;
 He blaws it east, he blaws it west,
 He blaws it whaur he liketh best.
Ma plaid awa, ma plaid awa,
An ower the hill an faur awa.

Anon.

8

Redeem Time Past

More oft than once Death whispered in mine ear,
Grave what thou hear'st in diamond and gold,
I am that monarch whom all monarchs fear,
Who hath in dust their far-stretch'd pride uproll'd;

All, all is mine beneath moon's silver sphere,
And nought, save virtue, can my power withhold:
This, not believed, experience true thee told,
By danger late when I to thee came near.

As bugbear then my visage I did show,
That of my horrors thou right use might'st make,
And a more sacred path of living take: –
Now still walk armèd for my ruthless blow:

Trust flattering life no more, redeem time past
And live each day as if it were thy last.

William Drummond of Hawthornden

9

Bedtime

The night comes down on foxes
As they run across the hill,
The night comes down on fallow deer
That wander where they will,

The night comes down on white owls
As they wake in the hollow trees,
The night comes down on badgers, free
To snuffle where they please,

The night comes down like velvet
On this house, and tenderly,
With starry streams and endless dreams
The night comes down on me.

Richard Edwards

10

A Toast

Here's tae ye a' yer days,
Plenty meat, an plenty claes;
Plenty parritch, an a horn spin,
An anither tattie when a's dune.

Anon.

11

Family Tree

My sister's mother's
husband's brother's
nephew's sister's
brother's . . . ME!

Lindsay MacRae

12

Winter Walk

Under a white skin of ice,
the river's clear veins push
air for sleeping fish.

Sun shatters on the hills'
blue spines, showers snow
with flashing dust.

In a dribbling cave we find
stone's slow tears
have made organ pipes of icicles,

a graveyard of unicorns.
You unroof two fluted horns
for your leaf-eyed head,

dance under armed trees.
I gather petticoats of starched web,
a blood-crown of cut haws.

Through many wind-shaped drifts
I hold your glove-furred paw
until air and fields blush.

Blue-breathed creatures let us stay
under these dragoned clouds
as birds' hearts flutter into silence,

the bloomed dusk falls,
under the knife of night;
the cold fires of space spark –

frozen in our own myth
with the moon veining our wooded path,
printing our feet with wildcat and deer.

Gillian Ferguson

13

In the Mid-Midwinter

after John Donne's 'A Nocturnal on St Lucy's Day'

At midday on the year's midnight
into my mind came
I saw the new moon late yestreen
wi the auld moon in her airms
though, no,
there is no moon of course –
there's nothing very much to speak of anything to speak of
in the sky except a gey dreich greyness
rain-laden over Glasgow and today
there is the very least of even this for us to get
but
the light comes back
the light always comes back
and this begins tomorrow with
however many minutes more of sun and serotonin.

Meanwhile
there will be the winter moon for us to love the longest,
fat in the frosty sky among the sharpest stars,
and lines of old songs we can't remember
why we know
or when first we heard them
will aye come back
once in a blue moon to us
unbidden
and bless us with their long-travelled light.

Liz Lochhead

A Winter Morning

At age 14, Ayrshire

Puddle ice cracked like lightbulb glass.
Frost had furred the last of the hips and haws.
My breath plumed out like a dragon's
In the cheering cold that morning the class
Was off for the day as the heating had failed –
Off for the week, with luck.

It was a gift, an escape from the wise laws
That governed things, a glimpse
Of possibility, like the thought
Of seeing a waxwing in an Irvine garden,
Or discovering a girl who liked you,
Or waking to find tremendous snow.
Not the escape itself, but its fine surprise.

Gerry Cambridge

15

Seize the Day

Come on, Daddy, come now I hear them shout
as I put the finishing touches to this and that

in the safe confines of my study:
Hurry, Daddy, before it's too late, we're ready!

They are so right. Now is the time.
It won't wait, on that you can bet your bottom

dollar. So rouse yourself, get the drift
before you're muffled and left

for useless. *Let's build a snowman, then
a snow-woman to keep him company. When*

*that's finished, and with what's left over,
a giant snow-ball that will last for ever,*

only hurry, Daddy. As soon as this poem
is finished, I promise, I'll come –

essential first, to pin down what is felt.
Meanwhile, the snow begins to melt.

Stewart Conn

16

Winter Bairns

Winter bairns are happed in snaw,
singing merrily on the brae.
Cauld aneuch the wind micht blaw,
it winna worry sic as they.

In this braw season, as they play
joyous as a burn in spate,
hardship takes a holiday
and winter bairns are never blate

at finding ferlies to create
or drawing dreams frae snaw and ice.
Skeely as they slide and skate
ye'd think they bade in paradise

and had nae thocht of puirtith's vice,
of cauld and hunger, fear and pain.
Whiteness makes the world seem wyce,
smoors owre ocht that isna clean.

With cranreuch cantie on the pane,
snaw drops sweetly, heaven-sent.
Winter's warmth is here again
and barefoot summer's lang ahint!

Donald Campbell

17

There will be no end

There will be no end to the joy, my love.
We will stand together as the stars
sweep the Cuillin, rounding into morning
the bright new morning of the tender heart.
And where we sing, the song will be a fine one
and where we dance, our steps will never fail
to tap the spring of life, of love and laughter
timeless as stars, the wheeling, circling stars
that dance and sing, and sing and dance again:
and there will be no end
to the joy

Anne MacLeod

18

Constant Love in All Conditions

Now doeth disdainfull Saturne sadd and olde
With ycie bearde enjoye his frosen raigne
His hoarie haires and snowie mantle colde
Ou'rcovers hills and everie pleasant plaine
While daez'd with frost, whiles droun'd with rapping raine
Doe beasts and birds bewaile there carefull cace
With longsume lookes in houpe to see againe
Sweet savoured Flora showe her aimeled face.

And looke how long they are in this estate,
This dolent season so there courage dants
That now no Cupide with his golden bate
Darr make there harts his harbour where he hants
Bot rather deade as are the trees and plants,
There spirits of life must hide them at the hart
Wherethrough there kindlie courage daylie scants
Whill mounting Phoebus make them to revert.

And shall I then like bride or beast forgett
For anie stormes that threatning heaven can send
That object sweete, wheron my hart is sett
Whome for to serve my senses all I bend
My inward flame with colde it dothe contend
The more it burnes, the more restrain'd it be
No winters frost, nor summers heate can end
Or staye the course of constant love in me.

King James VI

499

19

Christ Child's Lullaby

My love my pride my treasure oh
My wonder new and pleasure oh
My son, my beauty ever you
Who am I to bear you here?

Alleluia, alleluia,
Alleluia, alleluia.

The cause of talk and tale am I
The cause of greatest fame am I
The cause of proudest care on high
To have for mine the king of all

And though you are the King of all
They sent you to a manger stall
Then at your feet they all should fall
And glorify my child the King

Alleluia, alleluia,
Alleluia, alleluia.

There shone a star above three kings
To guide them to the King of Kings
They held you in their humble arms
And knelt before you until dawn

They gave you myrrh, they gave you gold
Frankincense and gifts untold
They travelled far these gifts to bring
And kneel before their newborn King

Alleluia, alleluia,
Alleluia, alleluia.

Father Ranald Rankin

20

The Computer's First Christmas Card

jollymerry
hollyberry
jollyberry
merryholly
happyjolly
jollyjelly
jellybelly
bellymerry
hollyheppy
jollyMolly
marryJerry
merryHarry
happyBarry
heppyJarry
bobbyheppy
berryjorry
jorryjolly
moppyjelly
Mollymerry
Jerryjolly
bellyboppy
jorryhoppy
hollymoppy
Barrymerry
Jarryhappy
happyboppy

boppyjolly
jollymerry
merrymerry
merrymerry
merryChris
ammerryasa
Chrismerry
asMERRYCHR
YSANTHEMUM

Edwin Morgan

21

The Yule Days

The King sent his lady on the first Yule-day,
A papingoe, aye.
Wha learns ma carol, an carries it away?

The King sent his lady on the second Yule-day,
Three pairtricks, a papingoe, aye.
Wha learns ma carol, an carries it away?

The King sent his lady on the third Yule-day,
Three plovers, three pairtricks, a papingoe, aye.
Wha learns ma carol, an carries it away?

The King sent his lady on the fourth Yule-day,
A goose that was grey,
Three plovers, three pairtricks, a papingoe, aye.
Wha learns ma carol, an carries it away?

The King sent his lady on the fifth Yule-day,
Three starlins, a goose that was grey,
Three plovers, three pairtricks, a papingoe, aye.
Wha learns ma carol, an carries it away?

The King sent his lady on the sixth Yule-day,
Three gowdspinks, three starlins, a goose that was grey,
Three plovers, three pairtricks, a papingoe, aye.
Wha learns ma carol, an carries it away?

The King sent his lady on the seventh Yule-day,
A bull that was broon,
Three gowdspinks, three starlins, a goose that was grey,
Three plovers, three pairtricks, a papingoe, aye.
Wha learns ma carol, an carries it away?

The King sent his lady on the eighth Yule-day,
Three ducks a-merry laying, a bull that was broon,
Three gowdspinks, three starlins, a goose that was grey,
Three plovers, three pairtricks, a papingoe, aye.
Wha learns ma carol, an carries it away?

The King sent his lady on the ninth Yule-day,
Three swans a-merry swimming, three ducks a-merry laying,
A bull that was broon,
Three gowdspinks, three starlins, a goose that was grey,
Three plovers, three pairtricks, a papingoe, aye.
Wha learns ma carol, an carries it away?

The King sent his lady on the tenth Yule-day,
An Arabian baboon,
Three swans a-merry swimming, three ducks a-merry laying,
A bull that was broon,
Three gowdspinks, three starlins, a goose that was grey,
Three plovers, three pairtricks, a papingoe, aye.
Wha learns ma carol, an carries it away?

The King sent his lady on the eleventh Yule-day,
Three hinds a-merry hunting, an Arabian baboon,
Three swans a-merry swimming, three ducks a-merry laying,
A bull that was broon,
Three gowdspinks, three starlins, a goose that was grey,
Three plovers, three pairtricks, a papingoe, aye.
Wha learns ma carol, an carries it away?

The King sent his lady on the twelfth Yule-day,
Three maids a-merry dancing, three hinds a-merry hunting,
An Arabian baboon,
Three swans a-merry swimming, three ducks a-merry laying,
A bull that was broon,
Three gowdspinks, three starlins, a goose that was grey,
Three plovers, three pairtricks, a papingoe, aye.
Wha learns ma carol, an carries it away?

The King sent his lady on the thirteenth Yule-day
Three stalks o' merry corn, three maids a-merry dancing,
Three hinds a-merry hunting, an Arabian baboon,
Three swans a-merry swimming, three ducks a-merry laying,
A bull that was broon,
Three gowdspinks, three starlins, a goose that was grey,
Three plovers, three pairtricks, a papingoe, aye.
Wha learns ma carol, an carries it away?

Anon.

22

Questions for Christmas

Will there be a child this year?
 Unexpectedly.

Are the wise men on their way?
 After a map-reading course.

Are the shepherds watching?
 As always.

Will the donkey nuzzle my hand?
 Sugar-lump or not.

Will there be snow and carols and an orange
at the bottom of my stocking and a Christmas tree?
 All of the above.

With lights?
 Clear ones.

Will there be love?
 Yes.

      Hamish Whyte and Diana Hendry

23

Old Christmastide

Heap on more wood! the wind is chill;
But let it whistle as it will,
We'll keep our Christmas merry still.
Each age has deem'd the new-born year
The fittest time for festal cheer:
Even, heathen yet, the savage Dane
At Iol more deep the mead did drain;
High on the beach his galleys drew,
And feasted all his pirate crew;
Then in his low and pine-built hall
Where shields and axes deck'd the wall
They gorged upon the half-dress'd steer;
Caroused in seas of sable beer;
While round, in brutal jest, were thrown
The half-gnaw'd rib, and marrow-bone:
Or listen'd all, in grim delight,
While Scalds yell'd out the joys of fight.
Then forth, in frenzy, would they hie,
While wildly loose their red locks fly,
And dancing round the blazing pile,
They make such barbarous mirth the while,
As best might to the mind recall
The boisterous joys of Odin's hall.

And well our Christian sires of old
Loved when the year its course had roll'd,
And brought blithe Christmas back again,
With all his hospitable train.
Domestic and religious rite
Gave honour to the holy night;
On Christmas Eve the bells were rung;
On Christmas Eve the mass was sung:
That only night in all the year,
Saw the stoled priest the chalice rear.
The damsel donn'd her kirtle sheen;
The hall was dress'd with holly green;
Forth to the wood did merry-men go,
To gather in the mistletoe.
Then open'd wide the Baron's hall
To vassal, tenant, serf and all;
Power laid his rod of rule aside
And Ceremony doff'd his pride.
The heir, with roses in his shoes,
That night might village partner choose;
The Lord, underogating, share
The vulgar game of 'post and pair'.
All hail'd, with uncontroll'd delight,
And general voice, the happy night,
That to the cottage, as the crown,
Brought tidings of salvation down.

The fire, with well-dried logs supplied,
Went roaring up the chimney wide;
The huge hall-table's oaken face,
Scrubb'd till it shone, the day to grace,
Bore then upon its massive board
No mark to part the squire and lord.
Then was brought in the lusty brawn,
By old blue-coated serving-man;
Then the grim boar's head frown'd on high,
Crested with bays and rosemary.
Well can the green-garb'd ranger tell,
How, when, and where, the monster fell;
What dogs before his death to tore,
And all the baiting of the boar.
The wassel round, in good brown bowls,
Garnish'd with ribbons, blithely trowls.
There the huge sirloin reek'd; hard by
Plum-porridge stood, and Christmas pie;
Nor fail'd old Scotland to produce,
At such high tide, her savoury goose.
Then came the merry makers in,
And carols roar'd with blithesome din;
If unmelodious was the song,
It was a hearty note, and strong.
Who lists may in their mumming see
Traces of ancient mystery;
White shirts supplied the masquerade,
And smutted cheeks the visors made;
But, O! what maskers, richly dight,
Can boast of bosoms half so light!

England was merry England, when
Old Christmas brought his sports again.
'Twas Christmas broach'd the mightiest ale;
'Twas Christmas told the merriest tale;
A Christmas gambol oft could cheer
The poor man's heart through half the year.

Sir Walter Scott

24

Balulalow

I come fra hevin here to tell
The best nowells that e'er befell
To you thir tythings trew I bring
And I will of them say and sing.
To you this day is born ane child
Of Marie meik and Virgin mild.
That blissit bairn bening and kind
Sall you rejoyce baith hart and mind.

O my deir hart, yung Jesus sweit,
Prepare thy creddil in my spreit!
And I sall rock thee in my hart
And never mair fra thee depart.
Bot I sall praise thee evermoir
With sangis sweit unto thy gloir.
The kneis of my hart sall I bow,
And sing that rycht Balulalow.

James, John and Robert Wedderburn

25

Child in the Manger

Child in the manger,
    Infant of Mary,
Outcast and stranger,
    Lord of all!
Child who inherits
    All our transgressions,
All our demerits,
    On him fall.

Once the most holy
    Child of salvation
Gentle and lowly
    Lived below;
Now as our glorious
    Mighty Redeemer,
See him victorious
    O'er each foe.

Prophets foretold him,
  Infant of wonder,
Angels behold him
  On his throne;
Worthy our Saviour
  Of all our praises;
Happy for ever
  Are his own.

Mary Macdonald,
translated by Lachlan Macbean

26

The Day After

The robin still comes
for his bread.

The reindeer
put their hoofs up
enjoy a mince pie.

Such a relief.
Cold turkey,
a black and white film.

Panto time.
Girls become boys,
boys dames. Peter flies.

The day-old baby
opens his eyes
to the world.

Hamish Whyte and Diana Hendry

27

On the thirteenth day of Christmas my true love phoned me up . . .

Well, I suppose I should be grateful, you've obviously gone
to a lot of trouble and expense – or maybe off your head.
Yes, I did like the birds – the small ones anyway were fun
if rather messy, but now the hens have roosted on my bed
and the rest are nested on the wardrobe. It's hard to sleep
with all that cooing, let alone the cackling of the geese
whose eggs are everywhere, but mostly in a broken smelly heap
on the sofa. No, why should I mind? I can't get any peace
anywhere – the lounge is full of drummers thumping
    tom-toms
and sprawling lords crashed out from manic leaping. The
kitchen is crammed with cows and milkmaids and smells
  of a million stink-bombs
and enough sour milk to last a year. The pipers? I'd forgotten
  them –
they were no trouble, I paid them and they went. But I can't
  get rid
of these young ladies. They won't stop dancing or turn the
  music down
and they're always in the bathroom, squealing as they skid
across the flooded floor. No, I don't need a plumber round,
it's just the swans – where else can they swim? Poor things,
I think they're going mad, like me. When I went to wash my

hands one ate the soap, another swallowed the gold rings.
And the pear tree died. Too dry. So thanks for nothing,
  love. Goodbye.

Dave Calder

28

The Tay Bridge Disaster

Beautiful Railway Bridge of the Silv'ry Tay!
Alas! I am very sorry to say
That ninety lives have been taken away
On the last Sabbath day of 1879,
Which will be remember'd for a very long time.

'Twas about seven o'clock at night,
And the wind it blew with all its might,
And the rain came pouring down,
And the dark clouds seem'd to frown,
And the Demon of the air seem'd to say –
'I'll blow down the Bridge of Tay.'

When the train left Edinburgh
The passengers' hearts were light and felt no sorrow,
But Boreas blew a terrific gale,
Which made their hearts for to quail,
And many of the passengers with fear did say –
'I hope God will send us safe across the Bridge of Tay.'

But when the train came near to Wormit Bay,
Boreas he did loud and angry bray,
And shook the central girders of the Bridge of Tay
On the last Sabbath day of 1879,
Which will be remember'd for a very long time.

So the train sped on with all its might,
And Bonnie Dundee soon hove into sight,
And the passengers' hearts felt light,
Thinking they would enjoy Old Year's Night
With their friends at home they lov'd most dear,
And wish them all a Happy New Year.

So the train mov'd slowly along the Bridge of Tay
Until it was about midway.
Then the central girders with a crash gave way,
And down went train and passengers into the Tay!
The Storm Fiend did loudly bray,
Because ninety lives had been taken away,
On the last Sabbath day of 1879,
Which will be remember'd for a very long time.

As soon as the catastrophe came to be known
The alarm from mouth to mouth was blown,
And the cry rang out all o'er the town,
Good Heavens! The Tay Bridge is blown down,
And a passenger train from Edinburgh –
Which fill'd all the people's hearts with sorrow,
And made them for to turn pale,
Because none of the passengers had liv'd to tell the tale
How the disaster happen'd on the last Sabbath day of 1879,
Which will be remember'd for a very long time.

It must have been an awful sight
To witness all this by dusky moonlight,
While the Storm Fiend did laugh, and angry did bray,
Along the Railway Bridge of the Silv'ry Tay.
Oh! ill-fated Bridge of the Silv'ry Tay,
I must now conclude my lay
By telling the world fearlessly without the least dismay,
That your central girders would not have given way,
Or so do many sensible people confess,
Had they been supported at each side with buttresses.
For the stronger we our houses do build,
The less chance we have of being killed.

William McGonagall

29

On the road

It's nearly New Year and we've loaded the van
with clothes for cold weather, boots and thick socks,
Christmas leftovers, the cat in a box,

and turn to the west. The fields are frozen
but rivers still run to the steely Forth.
The castle at Stirling floats on the carse,

and Ben Ledi's white head shoulders the blue
of a limitless sky. Ben Lomond borrows
light from the loch. At Rest and Be Thankful

the snow picks out the bones of the rock.
The mountains are darker, the sun at their back.
We're over the watershed, down to Cairndow.

Loch Fyne is like glass, and shows us the hills,
the curve of the shore and the lines of black trees
feathered in white, clear and still,

and there on the edge of this world, ourselves.
The wheels revolve, we've chosen the road.
We have to believe that we know where it goes.

Jenni Daiches

30

View of Scotland / Love Poem

Down on her hands and knees
at ten at night on Hogmanay,
my mother still giving it elbowgrease
jiffywaxing the vinolay. (This is too
ordinary to be nostalgia.) On the kitchen table
a newly opened tin of sockeye salmon.
Though we do not expect anyone,
the slab of black bun,
petticoat-tails fanned out
on bone china.
'*Last year it was very quiet . . .*'

Mum's got her rollers in with waveset
and her well-pressed good dress
slack across the candlewick upstairs.
Nearly half-ten already and her not shifted!
If we're to even hope to prosper
this midnight must find us
how we would like to be.
A new view of Scotland
with a dangling calendar
is propped under last year's,
ready to take its place.

Darling, it's thirty years since
anybody was able to trick me,
December thirty-first, into
'*looking into a mirror to see a lassie*
wi as minny heids as days in the year –'
and two already since,
familiar strangers at a party,
we did not know that we were
the happiness we wished each other
when the Bells went, did we?

All over the city
off-licences pull down their shutters,
people make for where they want to be
to bring the new year in.
In highrises and tenements
sunburst clocks tick
on dusted mantelshelves.
Everyone puts on their best spread of plenty
(for to even hope to prosper
this midnight must find us
how we would like to be).
So there's a bottle of sickly liqueur
among the booze in the alcove,
golden crusts on steak pies
like quilts on a double bed.
And this is where we live.
There is no time like the
present for a kiss.

Liz Lochhead

31

Auld Lang Syne

Should auld acquaintance be forgot
　　And never brought to mind?
Should auld acquaintance be forgot,
　　And auld lang syne?

Chorus
　　For auld lang syne, my dear,
　　　　For auld lang syne.
　　We'll tak a cup o' kindness yet,
　　　　For auld lang syne.

And surely ye'll be your pint stoup,
　　And surely I'll be mine;
And we'll tak a cup o' kindness yet,
　　For auld lang syne.

Chorus

We twa hae run about the braes,
　　And pou'd the gowans fine;
But we've wander'd mony a weary fit,
　　Sin' auld lang syne.

Chorus

We twa hae paidl'd in the burn,
    Frae morning sun till dine;
But seas between us braid hae roar'd
    Sin' auld lang syne.

Chorus

And there's a hand, my trusty fiere!
    And gie's a hand o' thine!
And we'll tak a right gude-willie waught,
    For auld lang syne.

Robert Burns

Glossary

a	I
a' / aa	all
a'm	I'm; I am
abeen	above
aboon	amongst; above
abune	upon
ach	ah; an expression of impatience, regret or annoyance. Sometimes used as a pause in a sentence
acquent	acquainted
ae	one, only
aff	off
afore	before
aft	often
agin	again
agley	awry
ahent / ahint	behind
aiblins	perhaps; possibly
aik	oak
ain	own
aipple	apple
airm	arm
airn / airns	iron / irons
airts	arts; skills
aits	oats
a-kaimin	a-combing
alane	alone
almus	almost
amang	among; amongst
ance	once
ane	one
anely	only
aneuch	enough
anither	another
ankers	anchors
aroon	around
ashet	oval serving plate or pie dish
assayit	experienced
astir	awake
athraw	awry
atween	between
auld	old
auld-farrant	old-fashioned; wise beyond years
Auld Nick	the Devil
ava	of all, above all
aw	all
awfie	awfully
awefu'	awful
awready	already
awthin'	everything
aye / ay	yes; always, ever, every
ayont	beyond
ba'	ball
bade	bid; also stayed, lived
bailie	provost; town-magistrate or official
bairn	child
bairnsang	children's songs; children's rhymes
baith	both
bandsters	binders
bane / banes	bone / bones
bard	a poet or minstrel
baudron	pussy-cat; affectionate term
bauld	bold
be	by; buy
bear	barley
beastes	beasts; cows
beastie	little beast
beir	bear; make
beld	bald
beldams	hags
believe / belyv	by-the-by
bels	pools
Beltane	1st May; an old Scottish quarter day; a pagan fire festival
beltit	surrounded; encircled; belted
ben	inside; towards, also mountain or hill
bening	benign; harmless
bethankit	thanks; Grace
bide	stay; reside
bidie-in	common-law partner
bield	refuge; shelter
big	build
billies	folks, people
birks	birches, birch trees

birl	twirl; revolve; twist; spin	**burdies**	birds; girls
birlin	revolving, spinning	**burn**	a small stream or brook, often at higher ground
bit	but		
bizz	buzz	**burr**	spear-thistle
blae	blue	**busk**	prepare; get ready
blaeberry	blueberry or bilberry	**buss**	bush
blate	bleat; sad; disappointed	**but**	without
blaw / blawn	blow / blown	**byke**	nest; beehive
bleeze	blaze	**by-ord'nar**	extraordinary
bleezing	blazing; alight	**ca'd**	called; put
bleiting	bleating	**cairn**	stone monument or rock pile
blellum	boastful or talkative man		
blest	blessed	**cals**	calls
blether	foolish chatter; gossip	**cam**	came
blethering	gossiping; rambling	**canna / cannae**	cannot; can't
blin's	blinds	**cannilie**	cannily
blindie	fool; drunkard	**canst**	can't
blissit	blessed	**cantie / canty**	pleasant; cheerful
bluid	blood	**cantraip**	magic; trickery
bluidy	bloody	**cark**	weight
bodie / body	person	**carlin**	witch
boddle	tuppence or farthing in old money	**Carlin Stone**	a prehistoric standing stone in Scotland, often associated with mythology and the supernatural
bogle / bogles	peek-a-boo; ghosts		
bonie / bonnie /	beautiful; handsome; fine-		
bony / bonny	looking	**castin**	casting
borraed	borrowed	**cauf**	calf
bore	gap, hiding place; shelter	**cauld**	cold
bosie	bosom; breast	**caur**	stoop; bow
bot	but	**ceilidh**	informal gathering amongst friends and neighbours, usually with song and the playing of instruments
bousing	boozing, drinking		
bout	bolt		
bow'd	bowed		
braes	grassy slope, hillside		
braid	broad; also bread	**chapmen**	peddlers, salesmen
braidit	braided; plaited	**chaumer**	chamber; room
braith	breath	**cheep**	chirp; sound
brak / brak's	break / breaks	**chiel**	young man
brast	bruised	**claes**	clothes
brattle	clatter	**claid**	clothed; covered
braw	fine; splendid; handsome	**claith**	cloth
breeks	trousers	**clamb**	climb; clamber
breid	bread	**clan**	a local or family group
brent	smooth; unwrinkled; brand new	**claucht**	caught; hooked; grasped
		claymore	a large, two-edged Highland sword
bricht	bright		
brither	brother	**cleadin'**	clothing
broach'd	brought; brewed	**cleare**	clear
broch	a prehistoric stone structure in the form of a tall, wide tower	**cleekit**	linked; latched; hooked
		cloit	sudden; heavy
		coft	bought
brocht	brought	**consentit**	consented
broo	brow	**coo**	cow
broon	brown	**coorie in**	cuddle in; snuggle up
bru / irn bru	a Scottish fizzy drink	**coost**	cast; threw down
bruckle	brittle; easily broken		
bughts	cattle pens		

coronach	a funeral lament or dirge, or a large outcry from a crowd
corrie	an armchair-like topographical feature, a hollow often found on Scottish mountainsides and common in Scottish place-names.
coulter	plough; blade
couplt	coupled
cowran'	cowering
cozie	cosy
cranreuch	hoar-frost
craws	crows, as in the bird. Can also mean gloating
creddil	cradle
creel / creils	basket / baskets for trapping fish
creeshie	greasy; oily
crie	call; talk
croon	crown
cruifs	wicker fish traps
crummock	stick; shepherd's crook
cud	could
cuif	rogue, fool
cum	come
curtsie	curtsy
cutty-sark	short underskirt
cuz	cousin; can also mean close
dae	do
daffin	foolish; light-hearted; tomfoolery
daimen	rare
darena	daren't
dauchter	daughter
dauner	stroll; saunter; wander
daur / daurna	dare / daren't
daurk	dark
daylicht	daylight
dee / deein'	die / dying
deep-doon	underground
deepe	deep
deil	devil
deip	deep
deir	dear
denner	dinner
dight	wipe
dinna / dinnae	don't
dirl	ring, vibrate
dis	does
disna	doesn't
dome	fate
dool	grief; distress
doon / doun	down

doosh	push; thud
dork	dark
dorty	sulky; haughty
douce	sweet; lovable or loving
dowie	sad
drave	drove
drear	dreary
dreepin	dripping; flowing
dreich	dreary; depressing
drookit	drenched; soaked
drouthy	thirsty
dub	mud
duddies	rags; tattered clothes
dug	dog
dune	done
durst	dare
dyke	low stone wall
e'e / een	eye / eyes
e'en	evening
eased	used
echt	eight
efter	after
eldritch	unearthly
ellys / na ellys	anything
emerant	emerald
endling	along
eneuch / enoo	enough
ensuin	coming; arriving
ettle	aim
ere	soon; until; before
es	ease
fa'	fall
fadom	fathom
faem	foam; sea spray
failyhe	fails
fain	gladly; affectionately; lust
fair fa'	fall well, good luck
fairin'	just desserts; what's coming
faither	father
fand	found
fareweel	farewell
fashious	troubling; inconvenient; bothersome
fast by	next to
faucht	fight; struggle
faulds	folds, layers
faur	far
fause	false
faut	fault
fechtin	fighting
feery-farry	a state of excitement or confusion
feit	feet
ferlie	curious; strange
festal	festive; feasting
fidg'd	fidgeted

fient	fiend	goun	gown
fiere	friend	gowan	daisy
fin	fine; well	gowden	golden
fir	for	gowdspink	goldfinch
fit	foot	gowk	a cuckoo bird. Can also
fitbaw	football		mean a fool or simpleton
flair	floor	gree	rank, grade
flang	kicked	greet	cry
flannen	flannel	greetin'	crying
flee	fly	grieve	provost, magistrate
flegs	blows; strikes	guid	good
flights	words	guidman	head of the table
flit	move	guidness	goodness
flitterin'	excited; flushed	guising	dressing up
flottered	spilled; overflowed	gurly	howling; roaring
fluidin	flooding, pouring	gyff	give
foggage	winter-grazing grass	ha' / haa	hall
forgie	forgive	haar	a cold mist or fog; an east
fou / fow	full; drunk		coast sea fog
frae / fre	from	hae / ha'e	have
freat / freit	superstitious	haena	haven't
frichted	frightened	haggis	a savoury meat pudding
froon	frown		with spices and oats,
fu'	full; full of		traditionally cooked
fu' brawlie	well-enough		and served in a sheep's
fur	for		stomach, usually eaten at
furst	first		Burn's Suppers
fy	yes; indeed	haiff	have
fyke	anxious, troubled; wrath	haiff-liking	pleasure
fyl'd	defiled; soiled	hailed	hauled
'ga / gae	go	hairt	heart
gabbin'	talking	hald	holding
gaed	went	hale	whole
gane	gone	hales	whole body; stature,
gang	go		appearance
gar'd	made	haly	holy
garb'd	worn; dressed	hame	home
gars	makes	hap	wrap
gat	get, got	happed	wrapped; covered;
gate	the way home		sheltered
gey	very; considerably	happity	lame; injured
ghaists	ghosts	harn	cloth
'gif / giffis	give / gives	har'st	harvest
gild	guild	hart	heart; also a stag
gin	if; whether	hauf	half
gled	glad	haugh	hock
glen	hollow; valley	haunfast	handfast; an engagement,
glisk	glimpse, glance; flash or		betrothal or wedding,
	twinkling		where the couple's union
glisterin	glittering; brilliant		is represented by the
gloamin' /	evening twilight; dusk		symbolic act of tying
gloaming			their hands together with
gloir	glory		material such as ribbon or
glow'rs	gazes intently		tartan
gonnae	going to	haup	hip
goon	gown	haurd	hard
goud / gowd	gold		

haws	hawthorn	kilt	tartan skirt-like garment
hear'st	hears; heard		traditionally worn by
heed	care		Highland Scottish men
heft	shaft	kirk	church
heid	head	kirn	churn; curds
heigh	high	kirtle	tunic; dress; garment
hen	an affectionate or familiar	kist	chest; storage trunk; a
	term for a girl or woman		large wooden box
het	hot	kittlin'	annoying; provoking;
heugh	precipice; ravine; cliff		tickling
hevin	heaven	knaw	know
hie / hies	call / calls	kneis	knees
hieland	Highland	knicht	knight
hind	hound	ky	cows
hinny	honey	kyte / kytes	belly / bellies
hirple	limp; hobble	lad	laid
hirsels	flock of sheep	lad / laddie	a young boy
histie	harvest; harvested	laids	loads
hollow	holler, shout	laigh	loop
hoo	how	laird	the landlord of an estate, a
hoose / hooise /	house		local chief or lord
housie		lairn'd	learned
horn	spoon	laith	loathe
hotch'd	jerked	Lammas	1st August; a Scottish
houlets	owls		quarter day
howe	hollow	lang	long
hud	had	lap	leaped
hurdies	buttocks	lass / lassie	a young girl
hus	has	lauch / leugh	laugh
i'	in	laverock	skylark
icker	ear of corn	Lawlands	Lowlands; the southern
ilk	this; that		parts of Scotland
ingle	fireplace	lea	field; pasture
intae	into	lea'e	leave
intil	into; inside	leal	loyal
ither / ithers	other / others	leamin	shiny, gleaming
jade	youth	learn	teach
jaups	splashes	leein'	sheltering
jeelie	jelly; fruit preserve or jam	leglin	footstool
jigging	carrying-on	levys	lives
jist	just	licht	light
Jo	love, sweetheart, darling	licht-hertit	light-hearted
Jock	the diminutive of John or	lichthoose	lighthouse
	Jack; a man	lichtlie	lightly
John Barleycorn	whisky	lift	sky
jouks	jumps; ducks, dodges	liftin	lifting
juist	just	lik	like
kame	comb	linket	danced
kend	knew	loch	a lake or large pond
keek	peek; look; glance	Loch Ness	a creature said in Scottish
kelpie	water demon in the form	Monster	folklore to live in the
	of a horse		deep waters of Loch Ness
kens	know / knows		in Invernessshire, the
kennin	knowing		Scottish Highlands
kent	knew / known	lochan	a small loch
kid-oan	pretend		

loon	young rascal (male); scoundrel
luggies	small wooden dishes
lugs	ears
luve / lo'e	love
lyart	grizzled
ma	my, mine
mair / mar	more
maircy	mercy
mairry	marry
maist	most
maitter	matter
masel	myself
maun	must
mavis	song-thrush
maw / ma	mother
meal-poke	beggar's bag; oatmeal bag
mebbe	maybe
meik	meek
meikle	huge
melder	period or quantity of milling corn
mibbe	maybe
micht	might
midge	a small flying insect, known for appearing in swarms in the north and west of Scotland during the summer months, and biting exposed skin
midnicht	midnight
'mid / 'midst	amid / amongst
mindin	memory, recollection
minds	reminds
minny	many
mire	bog
mirk	dark; gloomy; murk
mither	mother
Monenday	monday
moose / moosie / mousie / mousikie	mouse
mou	a large heap or pile, usually of grain
mourn'st	mourned
muckle	bulk; large amounts; a great deal
muircock	male red grouse
mumming	murmuring; mumbling
mune	moon
Munros	mountains in Scotland of 3,000 feet and over
mutch	close fitting cap
naig	horse, nag
nane	none
nannie	granddaughter
napp	wool
nappy	strong, foaming ale

neb	nose
neebor	neighbour
needna	needn't
neist	next
new-cutted	freshly-cut
nicht	night
nieve	fist
nigh	near
nit	nut
niver	never
no	not (e.g. I'm *no* doing that = I'm *not* doing that)
nocht / nought	nothing
noddle	head
noo	now
nor	than
norlan'	northerly
Noroway / Norroway	Norway
Nowells	noels
o / och	oh; an expression of impatience, regret or annoyance. Sometimes used as a pause in a sentence
oan	on
ocht	anything
ony / onie	any
onything	anything
oor	our
oorsel / oorsels	ourselves
oot	out
open	wild
outwith	outside or beyond, very commonly said in Scotland instead of these words
ower / owre	over; overly
owreheid	overhead
oxters	armpits
painch	stomach
pairtrick	partridge
papingoe	parrot
parritch	porridge
pattle	spade; plough-staff
pawkies	mittens; gloves
peat / peats	decayed and carbonised turf found in Scottish bogland countryside, often in the Highlands, and burned as fuel or used to insulate traditional houses
peedie	small; tiny
peelie-wally	sickly; pale
peerie	small; tiny creature
perfite	perfect

Glossary

perjink	precise; spotless; fastidious	sabbing	sobbing
perquer	perfect; perfectly	sae	so; also say
philibeg	little kilt	saft	soft
pibroch	traditional bagpipe music, usually for laments and salutes	sair / sairly	sore / sorely
		sall	shall
		sang / sangis	song
piece	a snack; a sandwich	sark	shirt; chemise; underclothes
pint stoup	pint cup; pint glass	Sassenachs	English-speaking, or non-Gaelic speaking Lowlanders of Scotland; commonly thought to be a term for English people south of the Scottish / English Border.
pits	puts		
pixie	bobble hat		
plaid	a length of tartan fabric		
planted	seated		
pollis	police		
poored	poured		
pou'd	picked	saul	soul
poussie	puss, pussy-cat	saut	salt
pouther'd	powdered	scanty	scarcely; hardly; limited
pow	head	scaur	sheer rock
press / presses	cupboard / cupboards	sconner	disgust
prys	prized	Selkirk Grace	a prayer said specifically before eating a Burns Supper
pu' / pu'ed / pu'd	pull / pulled		
puddin	sausage		
puir / puirer	poor / poorer	send	snap; cut off
puirtith	poverty	sett'st	sets
pund	pounds	shaw	thicket; natural wooded area
pussie	hare		
quaens	young girls	sheen	bright; beautiful
quait	quiet	sheiling	hut or collection of huts
quaten	quieten; suppress	sherp	sharp
queenis	queens	shinty	a Scottish stick and ball game similar to Irish hurling
quhilk	which; while		
race	rays		
rade	rode	shoggled	shook
rair	roar	shoon	shoes
rakin	raking; searching	shudny	shouldn't
rape	rope	shug-shugging	jog-jogging; swing-swinging
rapp'd	knocked		
rattlin	rattling	sic	such; suchlike
ravelin	unwinding; unravelling	siccan	such
reekit	smelled	sidie-ways	sideways
reel	a dance	silkie	a mythical creature taking both seal and human form, usually spelled selkie
reelin'	whirling; dancing		
reid / rid	red		
richt	right		
rigg(s)	row(s) in a field	simmer's	summer's
rigwoodie	gnarled; wizened	sin	since
rin / rins / rinnin'	run / runs / running	sine	then
ring	ramparts	skailin	scattering; spilling; dispersing
rive	burst		
rivin'	striding; ploughing	skarlet	scarlet
rosis	roses	skeely	skilled; trusty; capable
rowting	roaring; bellowing	skellum	rogue, scoundrel
rugging	pulling	skelp	slap; spank
rugs	pulls; tugs	skelpit	raced; belted
runkled	crumpled	skirl	squeal
rustic	rustic		

skinking	watery	tammy	woollen cap
skinklin	pouring;	tap	top
skitin'	sliding; send flying	tapmast	topmast
skoosh	spurt; splash; squirt	tattie	potato
skowts	large wet pile; sloppy mess	taul / tauld	told
skreech	screech	tell't	told
slap	wall	tentless	attentionless
Sleekit / Sleekit	smooth; sly; cunning; crafty	thae	they, those
		thair	there
sma'	small; slim; slender	thairm	intestines
smoor	smother; cover	thankit	thanked
smored / smoor'd	smothered; suffocated	thegither	together
sna	snow	them	those
snaw / snawy	snow / snowy	thi	the
snawdraps	snowdrops	thieve	steal
snell	sharp; biting; bitter	thir	their
socht	seek; sought	tho	though
sonsie / soncy	plump; round	thoctie	thought, notion
soom	swim; flood	thole	endure
souter	cobbler	thon	those, that
spake	spoke	thoosans'	thousands
spate	flood	thrave	a large measure of cut grain
spean	suckle; wean		
speer / speir	ask; inquire	thraw	throw
speldered	spread; sprawled	threid	thread
spindle shank	thin legs	threidit	threaded; woven
spreet / spreit	spirit	thro'	through
spune	spoon	thrums	threads; also purrs
stap	stop	thy-lane	alone
starlicht	starlight	thyrldom	enslavement
starr'd	starred; fated	tim'rous	timorous
staun / stauns	stand / stands	tint	lost
staw	sicken; steal / stole	tippeny	weak ale sold at two pence a pint
steeks	shuts		
stibble	corn	tirlin	pulling
stibble-field	corn-field	tod	fox
stoled	seated	toon / toun	town
stoure	strife; conflict; struggle	towzie	shaggy; scruffy
stovin'	steaming; stewing	treid	tread
straik	stroke	treisurs	treasures
strang	strong	trew	true
strath	river valley	troosers	trousers
strewin'	scattering	trow	true; believe
striv'n	strived	twa / twae	two
suld	should	twad	had; as if
sune	soon	'tweel	indeed
sunne	sun	'tween	between
sward	turf	tyke	dog
swat	sweat; sweated	tythings	tidings
swats	ales	unco	very much; greatly. Can also mean unfamiliar, strange
sweit	sweet		
syne	since; thereupon; directly after		
		unto	into
syped	seeped	uphaly	Christmastide; the end of the Festival of Epiphany
tae	to; across to. Can also mean toe		
		usquabae	whisky (*Gaelic: water of life*)
tae'en / ta'en	taken	vauntie	proud; vain; boastful

veesion	vision	**whissle**	whistle
vera / verra	very	**whit / whit's**	what / what's
wa'	wall	**whitever**	whatever
wad	would	**whyles**	sometimes
wadna	wouldn't	**wi'**	with
wae	we; also woe	**widd / wids**	wood / woods
waefu'	woeful	**wight**	valiant man
wage	pledge	**willie-waught**	hearty swig; usually of ale
waike	wake		or liquor
wairms	warms	**win'-cairdit**	wind-mapped; wind-
walie	ample		blown
waly	alas	**wing**	tale
wamblin	bouncing; wriggling	**win's**	winds
wan	lacking; defective, also	**winna**	won't
	won; one	**winnock**	window
wanlit	subdued; faded	**winnock-bunker**	window alcove; window
wap	throw; thrust; wrap		recess
wark	work; floor; ground	**wir**	our
warld / warl's	world / world's	**wis**	was
wast	west	**wisnae**	wasn't
wat	wet	**wist**	thought; wished; knew;
watchfu'	watchful		accounted for
water-wraith	an apparition; a warning	**withoot**	without
	sign of danger or	**without**	outside
	misfortune	**Wodensday**	Wednesday
watter	water	**woo'in**	wooing
wattergaw	rainbow	**wordy**	worthy
waukens	wakens	**wouldnae**	wouldn't
wauking	walking	**wrack**	wreck
wauknin	wakening	**wrang**	wrong
waukrife	wide-awake; vigilant;	**wud**	would
	unable to sleep	**wull**	will
wawlie	jolly	**wurld**	world
wean	baby, toddler, a small child	**wyce**	wise
weans / weanies	babies; children	**wyt**	wit; knowledge
wearilie	wearily	**ye**	you
wede	withered	**ye'll**	your
wee	small, little	**yer**	your
weet	wet	**yestreen**	yesterday evening
weill	well	**yet**	gate
wert	were	**yetts**	gates
westlin	westerly	**yharnt**	yearned; longed for
wey	way	**yin**	one
wha / wha's	who / who's	**yon**	that one; those over there
wham	which	**'yont**	beyond
whan	when	**younkers**	youngsters; young
whare	where		noblemen
wharfrae	where; where from		
whaup	curlew		
whaur / whaur's	where / where's		
wheech	whizz		
wheel	turn		
wheen	a good few; several		
wheesht	quiet		
whiles	whilst		
whin; whins	gorse; thorns		
whisht	quiet; silence		

Index of First Lines

Index of Authors and Translators

Acknowledgements

The compiler and publisher would like to thank the following for permission to use their copyright material:

Ace, Patricia: 'Skye Lines' from *Fabulous Beast* (Freight Books, 2013) by Patricia Ace. Copyright © Patricia Ace. Used with permission of the author **Ailes, Katie**: 'Outwith' by Katie Ailes. Copyright © Katie Ailes. Used with permission of the author. **Aitchison, James**: 'Anthem' from *The Gates of Light* by James Aitchison (Mica Press, 2016). Copyright © 2016. Reproduced by permission of Mica Press. **Askew, Claire**: 'Spitfires' from *This Changes Things* (Bloodaxe Books, 2016) by Claire Askew. Copyright © Claire Askew. Used by permission of the publisher. **Bateman, Meg**: 'Music in Church' and 'Ceòl san Eaglis' from *Soirbheas/Fair Wind* by Meg Bateman (Polygon, 2006). Copyright © Meg Bateman. Used with permission of the author. **Bissell, Norman**: 'Slate, Sea and Sky' from *Slate, Sea and Sky: A journey from Glasgow to the Isle of Luing* (Luath Press, 2015) by Norman Bissell. Copyright © Norman Bissell. Used with permission of the author. **Blackhall, Sheena**: 'The time traivellers' convention', 'The Only Bloody Hill in Scotland' and 'Haunfast' by Sheena Blackhall. Copyright © Sheena Blackhall. Used with permission of the author. **Bryan, Tom**: 'Scottish Rain' from *The Thing that Mattered Most: Scottish Poems for Children* (Scottish Poetry Library/ Black & White Publishing, 2006) ed. Julie Johnstone. Copyright © Tom Bryan. Used with permission from the author. **Buchan, Tom**: 'The Loch Ness Monster' from *Dolphins at Cochin* (Barrie & Rockliff/The Cresset Press, 1969) by Tom Buchan. Copyright © the Literary Estate of Tom Buchan. Used with permission of Lawrence Buchan on behalf of the Estate. **Burns, Elizabeth**: 'Sisters' from *Ophelia and other poems* (Polygon, 1991) by Elizabeth Burns, 'Grandmother' from *The Thing That Mattered Most: Scottish poems for children* (Scottish Poetry Library/Black & White Publishing) ed. Julie Johnstone and 'For W. S. Graham' from *The Gift of Light* (diehard, 1999) by Elizabeth Burns. Copyright © the Literary Estate of Elizabeth Burns. Used by kind permission of the Estate. **Burnside, John**: 'Two Saints' from *The Hoop* (Carcanet Press, 1988) by John Burnside. Copyright © John Burnside. Printed with permission of United Agents (www.unitedagents.co.uk) on behalf of John Burnside. **Calder, Dave**: 'Desk', 'Changed', and 'On the Thirteenth Day of Christmas' by Dave Calder from *Dolphins Leap Lampposts* (Macmillan Children's Books, 2002). Copyright © Dave Calder. Used with permission of the author. **Cambridge, Gerry**: 'The Stars of Autumn' from *The Shell House* (Scottish Cultural Press, 1995) by Gerry Cambridge and 'A Winter Morning' from *Madame Fi Fi's Farewell and Other Poems* (Luath Press Ltd, 2003) by Gerry Cambridge. Copyright © Gerry Cambridge. Used with permission of the author. **Cameron, Norman**: 'Shepherdess' from *Norman Cameron: Collected Poems and Selected Translations* (Anvil Press Poetry, 2011) by Norman Cameron. Copyright © the Literary Estate of Norman Cameron. Used with permission of the publisher. **Campbell, Angus Peter**: 'Belly-Button' and 'Eòin' by Angus Peter Campbell. Copyright © Angus Peter Campbell. Used with kind permission of the author. **Campbell, Niall**: 'The Work' from *Moontide* (Bloodaxe Books, 2014) by Niall Campbell. Copyright © Niall Campbell. Used with permission of the publisher. **Campbell, Donald**: 'Winter Bairns' from *Selected Poems* (Galliard, 1990) by Donald Campbell. Copyright © Donald Campbell. Used with permission of the author. **Carruth, Jim:** 'Farm Sale' from *Oxford Poets 2010* (Carcanet Press, 2010) ed David Constantine, Robyn Marsack and Bernard O'Donoghue. Copyright © Jim Carruth. Used with permission of the author. **Clanchy, Kate**: 'For a Wedding', 'Timetable' and 'Patagonia' from *Slattern* (Picador, 2001) by Kate Clanchy. 'The Bridge Over the Border' from *Samarka* (Picador, 2011) by Kate Clanchy. Copyright © Kate Clanchy. Used with permission of the publisher. **Clark, Thomas A.**: 'coire fhoinn lochan' and excerpt from 'Farm by the Shore' by Thomas A. Clark. Copyright © Thomas A. Clarke. Used with permission of the author. **Clark, Polly**: 'Friends' from *Farewell My Lovely* (Bloodaxe Books, 2009) by Polly Clark. Copyright © Polly Clark. Used by kind permission of the publisher. **Cleland, Angela**: 'Cross' from *Room of Thieves* (Salt Publishing, 2013) by Angela Cleland. Copyright © Angela Cleland. Used with permission of the author. **Cockburn, Ken**: 'Shandwick Stone' from *On the Flyleath* (Luath Press Ltd., 2007) by Ken Cockburn. Copyright © Ken Cockburn. Used with permission of the author. **Conn, Stewart**: 'Conundrum', 'Seize the Day' and 'Eclipse' from *A Touch of Time: New & Selected Poems* (Bloodaxe Books, 2014) by Stewart Conn. Copyright © Stewart Conn. Used with kind permission of the publisher. **Crawford, Robert**: 'Scotland' and 'Kiss' from *Full Volume* by Robert Crawford (Jonathon Cape, 2008). Copyright © Robert Crawford. Reprinted by permission of The Random House Group Limited. **Crichton Smith, Iain**: 'Love Poem' and 'River, River' by Iain Crichton Smith (Macdonald Publishers, 1978). Copyright © the Literary Estate of Iain Crichton Smith. Used with permission of Donalda Henderson on behalf of the Literary Estate. 'Luss Village' from *New Collected Poems* (Carcanet, 2011) ed. Matt McGuire. Copyright © the Literary Estate of Iain Crichton Smith. Used with permission of the publisher. 'Shores' from *From Wood to Ridge* (Carcanet, 1999) translation by Iain Crichton Smith. Copyright © the Literary Estate of Iain Crichton Smith. Used with permission from the publisher. **Daiches, Jenni**: 'On the Road' and 'Reading by a Window' by Jenni Daiches. Copyright © Jenni Daiches. Used with permission of the author. **De Luca, Christine**: 'Sooundscapes' first published in *Gutter #13* (Freight, 2015). Copyright © Christine De Luca. Used with permission of the author. **Dharker, Imtiaz**: 'Taal' from *Over the Moon* (Bloodaxe Books, 2014) by Imtiaz Dharker, 'Chaudri Sher Mobarik looks at a loch', 'Flight radar' and 'Six pomegranate seeds' from *Luck is the Hook* (Blooddaxe Books, 2018) by Imtiaz Dharker, 'Crab-Apple' and 'Seal, River Clyde' from *I Speak for the Devil* (Bloodaxe Books, 2001) by Imtiaz Dharker. Copyright © Imtiaz Dharker. Used with kind permission of the publisher. **Donaldson, Julia**: 'I Opened a Book' from *Crazy Mayonnaisy Mum* (Macmillan Children's Books, 2004) by Julia Donaldson. Extract from 'The Gruffalo' from *The Gruffalo Scots Edition* (Black & White publishing, 2012) by Julia Donaldson. Copyright © Julia Donaldson. Used with permission of the publisher. **Duffy, Carol Ann**: 'How Many Sailors to Sail a Ship' from *The Thing That Mattered Most* (Macmillan, 2006) ed Julie Johnstone and 'Prayer' from *Mean Time* (Anvil Press Poetry, 1993) by Carol Ann Duffy. Copyright © Carol Ann Duffy. Reproduced by permission of the author c/o Rogers, Coleridge & White Ltd., 20 Powis Mews, London, W11 1JN. **Dunn, Douglas**: 'One Renfrewshire Man to Another' by Douglas Dunn. Copyright © Douglas Dunn, 2018. Printed with permission of United Agents (www.unitedagents.co.uk) on behalf of Douglas Dunn. **Evanz, Sally**: 'Looking for Scotland' from *Looking for Scotland* (Salzburg, 1996) by Sally Evanz. Copyright © Sally Evanz. Used with permission of the author. **Ferguson, Gillian**: 'Orbit of Three' from *Baby* (Canongate Books ltd, 2001) by Gillian Ferguson and 'Winter Walk' from *Air for Sleeping Fishes* (Bloodaxe, 1997) by Gillian Ferguson. Copyright © Gillian Ferguson. Used with permission of the author. **Fitt, Matthew**: 'Fireworks aff the Castle' from *Goldfish Suppers* (Edinburgh City Council, 2004) by Matthew Fitt. Copyright © Matthew Fitt. Used with permission of the author. **Forrest-Thomson, Veronica**: 'I have a little nut tree' from *Collected Poems of Veronica Forrest-Thomson* ed. Anthony Barnett (Shearsman Books, 2008). Copyright © the Literary Estate of Veronica Forrest-Thomson. Used with permission from the Estate. **Fraser, Bashabi**: 'My mum's sari' from *The Thing That Mattered Most: Scottish Poems for Children* (Scottish Poetry Library/Black & White Publishing, 2006) ed. Julie Johnstone, *Primary KS1 and KS2 audio teaching resource* (Scholastic Resource) and *Poems Out Aloud* (Hodder Children's Books, 2003) chosen by Brian Moses. Copyright © Bashabi Fraser. Used with permission of the author. **Fraser, Douglas J.**: 'Highland Landscape' from *Landscape of Delight: Poems in Scots and English* (M. Macdonald, 1967) by Douglas J. Fraser. Copyright © the Literary Estate of Douglas J. Fraser. Used with permission of Heather Moncur on behalf of the Estate. **Frater, Anne**: 'Semaphore/Semaphore' by Anne Frater. Copyright © Anne Frater. Used with permission of the author. **Gibson, Magi**: 'Shh . . .' originally titled 'A Quiet Daughter' from *Graffiti in red lipstick* (Curly Snake Publishing, 2003) by Magi Gibson. Copyright © Magi Gibson. Used with permission of the author. **Gillies, Valerie**: 'Viking Boy' from *The Cream of the Well, New and Selected Poems* (Luath Press, 2014) by Valerie Gillies. Copyright © Valerie Gillies. Used with permission of the author. **Goldschmidt, Pippa**: 'Physics for the Unwary Student' from *House of Three: Logie Fielding vol. 2* (House of Three, 2016) by Pippa Goldschmidt and Nalini Paul. Copyright © Pippa Goldschmidt. Reprinted by permission of the author. **Gorman, Rody**: 'Fax/Fax' and 'Revolving Door/Doras-Cuartachaidh' from *Fax and Other Poems* (Polygon, 1996) by Rody Gorman. 'Hosai/Hosai' from *On the Underground* (Polygon, 2000) by Rody Gorman. 'Gazetteer' by Rody Gorman. Copyright © Rody Gorman. Used with permission of the author. **Gray, Alexander**: 'Scotland' and 'On a Cat, Ageing' from *Gossip: a book of new poems* (Porpoise Press,

1928) by Alexander Gray, and included in *Selected Poems* (William Maclellan, 1948) by Alexander Gray. Copyright © the Literary Estate of Sir Alexander Gray. Reproduced by permission of the Estate. **Hadfield, Jen**: 'Five Mackerel' and 'The Memory of Timber' from *Byssus* (Picador, 2014) by Jen Hadfield. Copyright © Jen Hadfield. Used with permission of the publisher. **Haggith, Mandy**: 'Listening to the Trees' from *letting light in* (Essence Press, 2005) by Mandy Haggith. Copyright © Mandy Haggith. Used with permission of the author. **Hendry, Diana**: 'Application' first published in *Handfast* (Scottish Poetry Library/Polygon, 2004) ed. Lizzie MacGregor. 'Streams' from *Strange Goings-On* (Viking, 1995) by Diana Hendry. 'Hiding Places' first published in *The Thing That Mattered Most: Scottish Poems for Children* (Scottish Poetry Library/Black & White Publishing, 2006) ed. Julie Johnstone. Copyright © Diana Hendry. Used with permission of the author. **Hendry, Diana and Whyte, Hamish**: 'Stars', 'Questions for Christmas' and 'The Day After' from *Green Fire & Bright Hopes: 12 Poems for Christmas* (Mariscat Press, 2014) by Diana Hendry and Hamish Whyte. Copyright © Diana Hendry and Hamish Whyte. Used with permission of the authors. **Herd, Tracey**: 'What I Wanted', 'What I Remember' and 'The Unicorn Seat' from *Not In This World* (Bloodaxe Books, 2016) by Tracey Herd. Copyright © Tracey Herd. Used by permission of the publisher. **Hershaw, William**: 'Songs of the Scottish Exam Board English Marker' and 'Turner Prize' from *The Cowdenbeath Man* (Scottish Cultural Press, 1997) by William Hershaw. Copyright © William Hershaw. Used with permission of the author. **Husband, Vicki**: 'On being observed' and 'Extremely Large Telescope' from *This Far Back Everything Shimmers* by Vicki Husband (Vagabond Voices, 2016). 'On being observed' first published in *Smiths Knoll #49* and *Be the First to Like This: New Scottish Poetry* (Vagabond Voices, 2014) ed. Colin Waters. Copyright © Vicki Husband. Used with permission of the author. **Jackson, Andy**: 'Enquiry Desk' first published in *Umbrellas of Edinburgh: Poetry and Prose Inspired by Scotland's Capital City* (Freight Books, 2016) ed. Claire Askew. Copyright © Andy Jackson. Used with permission of the author. **Jamie, Kathleen**: 'Deliverance', 'The Lighthouse', 'The Berries' and 'The Ponies' from *The Bonniest Companie* (Picador, 2015) by Kathleen Jamie. 'The Beach', 'The Stags', 'Fragment 1', 'Fragment 2' and 'The Whales' from *The Overhaul* (Picador, 2012). 'The Tay Moses' from *Jizzen* (Picador, 1999) by Kathleen Jamie. 'Crystal Set' by Kathleen Jamie. Copyright © Kathleen Jamie. Used with permission of the publisher. **Jarvie, Gordon**: 'Looking West, 'Skye Nocturne' and 'Walking the Botanic Gardens, Glasgow' from *A Man Passing Through: Memoir with Poems Selected and New* (Greenwich Exchange, 2016) by Gordon Jarvie. Copyright © Gordon Jarvie. Used with permission from the author. 'Cairngorm seedlings' from *Causeway/Cabhsair Magazine vol 8.1* (Aberdeen University Press, 2017). Copyright ©Gordon Jarvie. Used with kind permission of the author. **Kay, Jackie**: 'Gap year', 'Promise' and 'In My Country' from *Darling: New & Selected Poems* (Bloodaxe Books, 2007) by Jackie Kay. 'Small', 'Welcome Wee One', 'Rannoch Loop', 'Vault' and 'A Lang Promise' from *Bantam* (Picador, 2017) by Jackie Kay. 'Grandma's Soup' from *The* Frog Who Dreamed She Was an Opera Singer (Bloomsbury, 1998) by Jackie Kay. Copyright © Jackie Kay. Used by kind permission of the publishers and The Wylie Agency, Ltd on behalf of the author. **Lawrenson, Dorothy**: 'Viewmaster' by Dorothy Lawrenson. Copyright © Dorothy Lawrenson. Used with permission of the author. **Lochhead, Liz**: 'Kidspoem/ Bairnsang', 'Lankarshire Girls' from *The Colours of Black and White* (Birlinn Limited, 2003) by Liz Lochhead. 'The Teachers' and 'The Choosing' from *The Dreaming of Frankenstein* (Birlinn Limited, 2003) by Liz Lochhead. 'In the Mid-Midwinter' from *Fugitive Colours* (Birlinn Limited, 2017) by Liz Lochhead. 'View of Scotland / Love Poem' from *A Choosing: The Selected Poems of Liz Lochhead* (Birlinn Limited, 2017) by Liz Lochhead. Copyright © Liz Lochhead. Used with permission of the Licensor through PLSclear. **MacCaig, Norman**: 'Memorial', 'July Evening', 'Aunt Julia', 'Sounds of the Day', 'November Night, Edinburgh' and 'Basking Shark' from *The Many Days: Selected Poems of Norman MacCaig* (Birlinn Limited, 2010) by Norman MacCaig. Copyright © the Literary Estate of Norman MacCaig. Used with permission of the Licensor through PLSclear. **Mackay Brown, George**: 'Orkney – The Whale Islands', 'Island School', 'A Country Boy Goes To School' and 'Peat Cutting' from *Collected Poems* (John Murray Press, 2005) by George Mackay Brown. Copyright © the Literary Estate of George Mackay Brown. Reproduced by permission of John Murray Press, a division of Hodder and Stoughton Limited. **MacLeod, Anne**: 'Standing by Thistles' from *Standing by Thistles (Scottish Contemporary Poets)* (Scottish Cultural Press, 1997) by Anne MacLeod. Copyright © Anne MacLeod. Used with permission of the author. **MacNeil, Kevin**: 'All the Clouds', 'Faclan, eich-mhara/ Words, seahorses', 'Lost Loch Floating', 'The Harbour/An acarsaid' from *Love and Zen in Outer Hebrides* (Canongate Books, 1998) by Kevin MacNeil. Copyright © Kevin MacNeil. Used with permission of the author. **MacRae, Lindsay**: 'You Might as Well . . .', 'The Auntie with a Kiss Like a Heat-seeking Missile', 'Autistic', 'The Lost Word' and 'Family Tree' by Lindsay MacRae. Copyright © Lindsay Macrae. Used with kind permission of the author. **MacDiarmid, Hugh**: 'The Little White Rose' and 'Scotland' from *Complete Poems 2 vols.* (Carcanet Press, 1993) ed. Michael Grieve and W. R. Aitken. Copyright © Hugh MacDiarmid. Used with permission of the publisher. **Márkus, Gilbert**: 'Memorial of St Columba' original Latin from *Inchcolm Antiphoner* (14th century manuscript in Edinburgh University Library) translated by Gilbert Márkus. Copyright © Gilbert Márkus. Used with kind permission of the translator. **McCarey, Peter**: 'You've got fifteen seconds in which to' and 'Unachievable Hopes' from *Collected Contraptions* (Carcanet Press, 2011) by Peter McCarey. Copyright © Peter McCarey. Used with kind permission of the publisher. **McGonigal, James**: 'Kneehigh to a Poem' by James McGonigal from *Macmillan Scottish Poems* (Macmillan Children's Books, 2001) chosen by John Rice. Copyright © James McGonigal. Used with kind permission of the author. **McSeveney, Angela**: 'Be-Ro' from *Slaughtering Beetroot* (Mariscat Press, 2008) by Angela McSeveney. 'Windowbox' from *Coming Out With It* (Polygon, 1992) by Angela McSeveney. 'Who's Who' from *Imprint* (Edinburgh Review, 2002) by Angela McSeveny. Copyright © Angela McSeveney. Used with permission from the author. **Meade, Gordon**: 'The Song of the Grasshopper' first appeared in *A Man at Sea* (diehard,

2003) by Gordon Meade. Copyright © Gordon Meade. Used with permission of the author. **Mitchell, Elma**: 'Recreation', 'Life-Cycle of the Moth', 'It's the Sea I Want' from *The Human Cage* (Peterloo Poets, 1979) by Elma Mitchell. 'This Poem . . . ' and 'People Etcetera' from *People Etcetera: Poems New & Selected* (Peterloo Poets, 1987) by Elma Mitchell. Copyright © the Literary Estate of Elma Mitchell. Used with permission of Hannah Elliot on behalf of the Estate. **Morgan, Edwin**: 'Slate', 'The Loch Ness Monster's Song', 'Particle Poems: 3', 'Midge' and 'The Computer's First Christmas Card' from *Collected Poems* (Carcanet Press, 1997) by Edwin Morgan. Copyright © the Literary Estate of Edwin Morgan. Used with kind permission of the publisher. **Morgan, J. O.**: 'We used to think the universe was made . . .' from *Interference Pattern* (Jonathon Cape, 2016) by J. O. Morgan. Copyright © J. O. Morgan. Reprinted by permission of The Random House Group Limited. **Muir, Edwin**: 'The Northern Islands', 'The Confirmation' and 'A Birthday' from *Collected Poems* (Faber and Faber Ltd, 2003) by Edwin Muir. Copyright © the Literary Estate of Edwin Muir. Used with permission of the publisher. **Muñoz, Theresa**: 'Be the first to like this' first published in *Gutter #8* (Freight, 2013). Copyright © Theresa Muñoz. Used with permission of the author. **Murray, Donald S.**: 'An Incomplete History of Rock Music in the Hebrides' by Donald S. Murray. Copyright © Donald S. Murray. Used with permission of the author. **O'Rourke, Donny**: 'Great Western Road' first published in *New Writing Scotland: Some Sort of Embrace No.15* (Association for Scottish Literary Studies, 2001) ed. Kathleen Jamie and Donny O'Rourke. Copyright © Donny O'Rourke. Used with permission of the author. **Paterson, Don**: 'Three Lyrics' from *The Eyes* (Faber, 1999) by Don Paterson. Copyright © Don Paterson. Reproduced by permission of the author c/o Rogers, Coleridge & White Ltd., 20 Powis Mews, London W11 1JN. **Paterson, Stuart A.**: 'Almorness' by Stuart A. Paterson. Copyright © Stuart A. Paterson. Used with permission of the author. **Paulin, Dorothy Margaret**: 'A Galloway Burn in June' and 'December Day' by Dorothy Margaret Paulin. Copyright © the Literary Estate of Dorothy Margaret Paulin. Used with permission of Maggi Kaye on behalf of the Estate. **Pedersen, Michael**: 'Hello, I am Scotland' from *Oyster* (Polygon, 2017) by Michael Pedersen. Copyright © Michael Pedersen. Used by kind permission of the author. **Poleg, Stav**: 'I'm sending you a letter' from *Lights, Camera* (Eyewear Publishing, 2017) by Stav Poleg. Copyright © Stav Poleg. Used with permission of the author. **Pow, Tom**: 'Crabs: Tiree' from *In the Becoming – New and Selected Poems* (Polygon, 2009) by Tom Pow. Copyright © Tom Pow. Used with permission of the agent. **Price, Richard**: 'The World is Busy' from *Lucky Day* (Carcanet Press, 2005) by Richard Price. Copyright © Richard Price. Used with permission of the publisher. **Ransford, Tessa**: 'Blake's Wife' from *When it Works it Feels like Play* (Ramsay Head Press, 1998) by Tessa Ransford. 'March Weather' from *Made in Edinburgh* (Luath Press Ltd, 2014) by Tessa Ransford. Copyright © the Literary Estate of Tessa Ransford. Both used with permission from Hilda Stiven on behalf of the Literary Estate of Tessa Ramsford. **Riach, Alan**: 'Ossian's Grave' from *The Winter Book: New Poems* (Luath Press Ltd., 2017) by Alan Riach and 'The Blues' by Alan Riach. Copyright

© Alan Riach. Used with permission of the author. **Rice, John**: 'A Minute to Midnight', 'Driving at Night with My Dad', 'Climbing the World', 'Constant, Constant Little Light', 'Scottish Haiku', 'Dreamscape at Bedtime', 'Dazzledance', 'Follow the Rainfall', 'The Fairy School Under the Loch' by John Rice. Copyright © John Rice. Used with kind permission of the author. **Robertson, James**: 'Doctor Wha' from *Where Rockets Burn Through* (Penned in the Margins, 2012) ed. Russell Jones, Edwin Morgan and Joe Dunthorne. Copyright © James Robertson. Used with permission of the author. **Rowling, J. K.**: 'The Sorting Hat Song' from *Harry Potter and the Philosopher's Stone* (Bloomsbury, 1997) by J. K. Rowling. Copyright © J. K. Rowling. Used with permission of The Blair Partnership on behalf of the author. **Shepherd, Nan**: 'Spring', 'Summit of Corrie Etchachan' and 'The Hill' from *In the Cairngorms* (Galileo Publishers, 2014) by Nan Shepherd. Copyright © Galileo Publishers. Used by permission of the publisher and the Literary Estate of Nan Shepherd. **Spark, Muriel**: 'Litany of Times Past' from *All the Poems of Muriel Spark* (New Directions, 2004) by Muriel Spark. Copyright © 2004 by Muriel Spark. Used with permission of Georges Borchardt, Inc. on behalf of the author. **Steven, Kenneth C.**: 'Grey Geese' by Kenneth C. Steven. Copyright © Kenneth C. Steven. Used with permission of the author. **Stevenson, Gerda**: 'Queen o the Bean', 'Teneu', '"Columbine" Cameron', 'Nine Haiku for Esther Inglis' and 'Saint Margaret' from *QUINES: Poems in tribute to women of Scotland* (Luath Press Ltd., 2018) by Gerda Stevenson. Copyright © Gerda Stevenson. Used with permission of the author. **Sulter, Maud**: 'If Leaving You' by Maud Sulter. Copyright © the Literary Estate of Maud Sulter. Permissions courtesy of the Estate of Maud Sulter, 2018-2020. **Tait, Margaret**: 'To Anybody At All' by Margaret Tait. Copyright © the Estate of Margaret Tait. Reprinted courtesy of the Orkney Library and Archive and the Margaret Tait Estate. **Thornton, Valerie**: 'The Cat's Tail' from *Catacoustics* (Mariscat, 2000) by Valerie Thornton. Reprinted in *Scottish Poems* ed. John Rice (Macmillan Children's Books, 2001). Copyright © Valerie Thornton. Used with permission of the author. **Tongue, Samuel**: 'Oak Branch and Tree Warbler' from *Hauling-Out* (Eyewear, 2016) by Samuel Tongue. Copyright © Samuel Tongue. Used with kind permission of the author. **Watt, Nuala**: 'Untitled' by Nuala Watt. Copyright © Nuala Watt. Used with permission of the author. **Whyte, Hamish**: 'Hop and Hope', 'Sound Like' and 'Letter from a Spring Garden' from *Now the Robin* (HappenStance, 2017) by Hamish Whyte. 'Appointment' first published in *Handfast: Scottish Poems for Weddings and Affirmations* (Polygon, 2014) ed. Lizzie McGregor. Copyright © Hamish Whyte. Used with permission of the author. **Young, Alan**: 'For as Long as' by Alan Young. Copyright © Alan Young. Used with permission of the author.

Every effort has been made to trace the copyright holders, but if any have been inadvertently overlooked the publisher will be pleased to make the necessary arrangement at the first opportunity.

Thanks

This book would not have happened without the brilliant Cate Augustin and Simran Sandhu. Their calm in the face of *so* many poems and general loveliness has made making this book an utter joy from start to finish.

For Grant, Jude and Evie who are still on a road trip to Scotland with me! To quote Diana Gabaldon 'That's the first law of thermodynamics' xx

So many excellent people have helped with this book – suggesting poets, reading drafts, tracking down permissions holders and generally being really enthusiastic. Thanks to everyone at the Scottish Poetry Library – especially Emily Prince and Gillian Hamnett – Jackie Kay, John Rice, Hamish Whyte, Stewart Conn, Gordon Jarvie, Gillian MacKay, Nick de Somogyi, Tracey Ridgewell, Cheyney Smith, Suzanne Fairless-Aitken, Foichl Miah, Josie Shenoy and The Dimpse.

About Gaby Morgan

Gaby Morgan is an Editorial Director at Macmillan Children's Books. She has compiled many bestselling anthologies including *Read Me and Laugh: A Funny Poem for Every Day of the Year*, *Poems from the First World War*, *Fairy Poems* – which was short-listed for the CLPE Award – and *A First Poetry Book* with Pie Corbett. She is happiest at the seaside.